A FIREFLY BOOK

Copyright © 2008 Oio Editions

Published in the United States & Canada by Firefly Books Ltd

First printing

Publisher Cataloging-in-Publication Data (U.S.)

Marçais, Nicolas.
    Crazy stuff / Nicolas Marçais ; Philippe Marchand.
[416] p. : col. photos. ; cm.
Includes index.
Summary: Strange and unusual new products from low-tech oddities, to high-tech time savers.
ISBN-13: 978-1-55407-426-6
ISBN-10: 1-55407-426-6
1. Curiosities and wonders. 2. Technology – Miscellanea. 3. Inventions – Miscellanea. 4. Commercial products – Miscellanea. I. Marchand, Philippe. II. Title.
609 dc22   T45.M373   2008

Library and Archives Canada Cataloguing in Publication

Marçais, Nicolas
    Crazy stuff / Nicolas Marçais and Philippe Marchand.
Includes index.
ISBN-13: 978-1-55407-426-6
IBN-10: 1-55407-426-6
1. Material culture. 2. Popular culture. 3. Civilization, Modern — 21st century. 4. Twenty-first century. I. Marchand, Philippe II. Title.
CB430.M365 2008   306   C2008-903447-3

Published in the United States by
Firefly Books (U.S.) Inc.
P.O. Box 1338, Ellicott Station
Buffalo, New York 14205

Published in Canada by
Firefly Books Ltd.
66 Leek Crescent
Richmond Hill, Ontario L4B 1H1

A concept and a selection by
Nicolas Marçais & Philippe Marchand

Editor
Nicolas Marçais

Designer
Philippe Marchand

Writers
Anne Kerloc'h
Sarah Jean-Marie
Chantal Allès
Sophie Hazard
Delphine Blanchet
Nicolas Marçais

Image creation & Page-setting
Fanny Naranjo

Photo research
Etienne Bréchignac
Nicolas Schmaltz

Translated from the French by
Mark Neimeyer

Printed in Thailand by Imago

Note: All dollar amounts are in USD.

crazy stuff

Nicolas Marçais
Philippe Marchand

FIREFLY BOOKS

They should invent something that... Just imagine if there was... If only... Forget all that hypothetical thinking. It's already been invented and produced, and it's available at your local neighborhood supplier of dreams and other silly gadgets. Don't believe it? Look on page 24. Or 37. Or any other page in this book. There's now an air conditioner for the brain, a camera for your cat, a fake smile for your dog, and even a hotel on the moon for regular old human beings. And these things didn't escape from some bizarre novel. They really exist in our wonderful, zany world. Surprising, clever and sometimes totally absurd, the ideas and objects in *Crazy Stuff*, in their own unique way, tell the story of our lives in today's global village. They provide unusual answers to questions we hadn't even thought of, taking us along unexplored paths and leading us to places far off the beaten track. It's in these isolated regions of our world and in our minds, these chinks in our universe, that humanity reinvents itself. Some of the things presented here will no doubt be quickly forgotten. But others may very well become part of our everyday lives in a future that's just around the corner.

Life is a strange and magnificent journey. This book is dedicated to those who enjoy being surprised by it.

crazy places

Sometimes it seems as though there's nothing left to discover in this world. We've known that it's not flat for quite some time now, and most of the barriers that once existed have come tumbling down, allowing some of us to fly from country to country the way others hop on a bus. Are there no new frontiers? No unusual places that haven't been seen before? In fact, they're all around us, and there are new ones every day. You just have to start exploring, and you just might find a hotel hidden inside a drainpipe. Or a little port named Dubai, which has become a bridge toward the future and a new kind of urban living — bringing together the earth, the sea and the sky. And what about further out? Soon space will become a playground for tourists looking forward to zero gravity evenings and beautiful views of our blue planet, paying for their galactic thrills with moon money. Every day, the stars are getting closer, and the sky is becoming more familiar. But even when humans have traveled to the far reaches of the solar system and beyond, there'll still be another unknown world to investigate — the one beyond the grave. This time, however, you won't be able to tell your friends about the journey, because death is still a wild, untamed region, and they're not selling any round-trip tickets there. As you leave for this final passage, however, there's no reason why you can't do it with a little bit of imagination and style — one last little fling for the closing act.

The Sleepover Museum

The active and fertile imagination of German artist Lars Stroschen has no limits. Everything gets him excited — images, sounds, materials, you name it. With the Propeller Island City Lodge, Berlin, he's found a place where he can really express himself. The 30 rooms are all different, but they have one thing in common: they each give their occupants the opportunity to live in a genuine work of art. The decoration, furniture and objects in the rooms are unique and were all designed and created by Stroschen. Propeller Island is a veritable art museum — where you can stay overnight.

Did you know?

Propeller Island City Lodge takes its name from one of the novels in Jules Verne's *Extraordinary Voyages* series.

Propeller Island City Lodge
PRICE: **FROM $85 TO $167 A NIGHT**
Information: **http://www.propeller-island.de**

The Deluxe Igloo

The Swedes don't only make furniture you have to put together yourself — they also make hotels out of ice cubes. Each year, in the middle of November, a team of architects and construction workers head about 120 miles (193 km) north of the Arctic Circle to build an ice hotel. Since they have to start from scratch each time, it's never exactly the same from year to year. But if you don't like the cold then this place is definitely not for you. From the hotel entrance right to your bed, everything is made of blocks of frozen water from the River Torne. And don't think you're going to warm yourself up with a nice cup of mulled wine. They don't serve hot drinks at the bar because they'd melt the glasses — which are also made of ice. You'll just have to settle for vodka.

Did you know?

The Ice Hotel has a chapel where you can get married. And with its icy white décor, your love will stand out as your warmest memory. There are also ice hotels in Finland (http://www.snowcastle.net) and Canada (http://www.icehotel-canada.com).

Ice Hotel
PRICE: **FROM $172 TO $771 A NIGHT**
Information: **www.icehotel.com**

A Room with a View

Water as far as you can see, and seagulls ruling the skies — it's the perfect vacation for anyone who loves the outdoors and hates crowds. Staying overnight in a Norwegian lighthouse is the perfect way to enjoy a truly exceptional view in a magical atmosphere, and your only neighbors will be the wind and the birds. A few of these lighthouses are totally isolated and can only be reached by boat.

Did you know?

Some of the lighthouses are pretty basic, equipped with bunk beds and a simple kitchenette. Others are truly deluxe accommodations, like the Krakenes lighthouse, which offers a bridal suite in the loft of the main building.

Lighthouse hotels
PRICE: **FROM $46 TO $145 A NIGHT**
Information: **http://www.visitnorway.com**

Up on the Rooftop

It's been here and there, moving around Europe. From museums to roofs, the Everland Hotel wanders around. In 2002 it was taking in the fresh air at Lake Neuchâtel during the Swiss National Exhibition. It's been seen on top of the Leipzig Gallery of Contemporary Art in Germany. In December it moved to the roof of the Palais de Tokyo museum in Paris. There, guests will be able to experience a night that gives its full meaning to the "City of Light." In fact, this nomadic room is actually a contemporary art installation created by the duo Sabina Lang and Daniel Baumann. People who spend the night in the Hotel Everland become part of the work of art and are invited to participate in its creation, including by helping themselves to the minibar and stealing the embroidered towels when they leave.

Did you know?

Everland is only available for one night at a time, in order to maximize the number of participants in the project. Each date is put on sale on a specific day, but at a time chosen at random. A few lucky — and enterprising — buyers have resold their nights at Everland on eBay for up to $5,800.

Everland
PRICE: **FROM $483 TO $644 A NIGHT**
Information: **http://www.everland.ch**

The Sky Crane

There are tourists sleeping in Harlingen Harbour — in the comfort of a silent crane. From the 1960s until the 1990s it was used to unload timber from cargo ships in this Dutch port. In 2003 the crane was transformed into a deluxe hotel. Since it only has one room, perched about five stories above the ground atop spidery metal legs, you can have the Harlingen Harbour Crane all to yourself. Far from the madding crowd — and close to the fresh sea air — you can enjoy a spectacular view from its two levels of terraces and its bay windows. And if you want a change of scenery, all you need to do is climb up into the operator's cabin. With a simple movement of the control stick, you can rotate your room 360 degrees for a panorama you'll never get tired of. Breakfast is delivered by one of the two modern elevators added during the renovations.

Harbour Crane
PRICE: **FROM $463 A NIGHT**
Information: **http://www.vuurtoren-harlingen.nl**

The Ginormous Swimming Pool

If you like to vacation by the sea but you want to avoid the waves and the unseen dangers of the deep, now you can — at the biggest swimming pool in the world. In 2006 a hotel complex in Chili, San Alfonso del Mar, hired the Crystal Lagoons Corporation to create a 20-acre (8 ha) artificial lake that contains over 600,000 gallons (2.5 million) of constantly filtered saltwater, maintained at a warm 80°F (26°C). Over half a mile (1 km) long, it's large enough for windsurfing or kayaking. And there's even a water-bus to help you get around.

Did you know?

The lagoon, which figures in the *Guinness Book of World Records*, is as big as 50 Olympic-size swimming pools or about 6,000 typical private pools.

San Alfonso del Mar
PRICE: **FROM $1,300 A WEEK**
Information: **www.sanalfonso.cl**

The Salt Hotel

In Bolivia, next to the world's largest salt flat, they know how to make the most of their resources. A tiny part of the tens of millions of tons of salt has been used to build... a hotel. With 23 rooms, the Luna Salada Hotel is constructed entirely out of bricks made from a salt and water mixture. Even the furniture — tables, chairs, beds, everything — is made of salt. And as long as you don't lick the walls it's compatible with a low-sodium diet.

Did you know?

The hotel has a certain rustic charm, and accommodations are a bit rudimentary. Translucent corrugated sheets are placed over the beams of open parts of the ceiling to provide protection from rain, and the hotel is not heated, which can take away just a little bit of the place's magic, since at night temperatures can drop close to freezing.

Luna Salada
PRICE: **FROM $72 A NIGHT**
Information: **http://www.lunasaladahotel.com.bo/en.html**

Jungle fever

Discover the Amazon in a new way — and with the whole family. The Ariaù Amazon Towers hotel complex offers accommodations ranging from standard rooms to suites to the ultimate jungle experience, their Tarzan Houses, all of which are perched in the trees, about 30 feet (9 m) above the ground. The hotel offers different tour packages to help you discover the region, including river cruises, alligator and piranha spotting, hikes in the rain forest, encounters with monkeys and exotic birds, visits to nearby villages and opportunities to sample the local cuisine.

Ariaù Amazon Towers
PRICE: **FROM $200 TO $3,000 A NIGHT**
Information: **http://www.ariautowers.com**

Ewok Revival

Why not live like the Swiss Family Robinson? The Finca Bellavista community offers you a truly unusual lifestyle, in total harmony with nature. For several years this community, located in Costa Rica, has been building tree houses designed for year-round residences or as vacation homes. The concept was inspired by the Ewok village in the Star Wars film *Return of the Jedi*. There are simple accommodations on site where you can stay while looking at the parcels of land available. You can build as simple or as luxurious a tree house as you want, or just leave the land undeveloped and help preserve the rain forest. You can't drive your car around this community, but ground trails and modern rope bridges in the rain forest canopy allow you to get around and visit the neighbors. And modern civilization does have its place here: since 2008 the tree houses have had high-speed Internet access powered by solar energy.

Finca Bellavista
PRICE: **TREE HOUSES CAN BE BUILT FROM $10,000 TO $50,000**
Information: **http://www.fincabellavista.net**

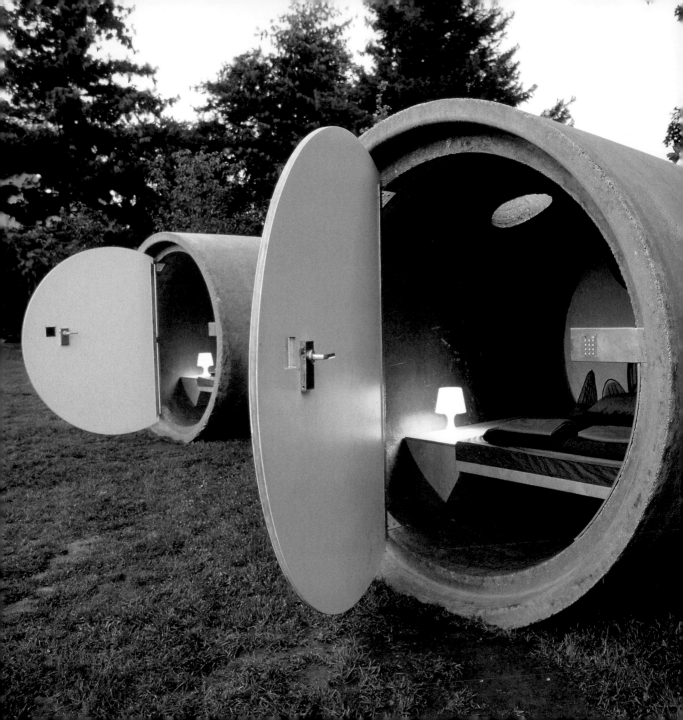

The Pipedream Hotel

The Greek Cynic philosopher Diogenes lived in a tub. So why not stay overnight in a drainpipe? That's exactly what you can do at Das Park Hotel in Ottensheim, Austria. These hotel rooms — which from the outside do nothing to hide the fact that they're actually giant concrete pipes — are actually quite comfortable. Each one is equipped with a double bed, warm blanket, bedside lamp, storage space and colorful mural. The lock works with a code you receive in advance by e-mail, so you can arrive any time you want. As for a minibar, shower or toilet, you're going to have to venture out into the park and the nearby town center to take care of those needs. But for the price, you really can't complain, because at Das Park Hotel, not only do you get a good night's sleep, but you pay whatever you want.

Did you know?

The Das Park Hotel is located in Ottensheim, Austria, right near the Danube.

Das Park Hotel
PRICE: **WHATEVER YOU WANT**
Information: **http://www.dasparkhotel.net**

A Capsule a Day

You leave your bags on a shelf at the reception desk and put your clothes in a metal locker before hitting the showers. But this isn't a sports club — it's a hotel. Capsule hotels have become fairly common in Japan, especially in big cities where every square inch counts. The capsules themselves are basically rectangular boxes, about 6½ feet (2 m) deep, stacked on top of one another. With a height and width of about 2½ feet (75 cm), there's barely enough room to sit up, but that doesn't matter because you're there to sleep. A large percentage of the clientele is made up of businesspeople working late. And the sexes are segregated, which reduces your chances of being kept awake by the couple next door.

Did you know?

Capsule hotels do offer a certain level of comfort: the sheets and towels as well as the bathrooms are as clean as in a hospital — and each capsule has a television.

Capsule Inn
PRICE: **ABOUT $40 A NIGHT**
Information: **http://www.capsuleinn.com**

525

Safe and Sound

Free the artist inside you — at the Celica Hostel in Ljubljana, Slovenia. This unique place to stay offers a luxurious getaway in a charming prison cell. The rooms aren't very big, but you won't be coming here to play cops and robbers or warden and prisoner. The service is excellent, and 20 cells of this former penitentiary, from number 101 to 120, have been renovated by contemporary artists. It's like a series of suggestions in an article on "how to make the most of a small space" in *House Beautiful* — with just a touch of black humor. In number 111 there's a simple bed on a brick and wood base built into the corner, for that rustic touch; in number 114 there are exposed beams and a pebble floor. It might take some time, however, to get used to the bars on the windows.

Celica Hostel
PRICE: **FROM $26 TO $39 A NIGHT**
Information: **http://www.hostelcelica.si**

Beyond Modern

The Hotel Puerta América in Madrid is a tribute to art and diversity. The facade, the bars and lounges, the parking garage, the main lobby, the gardens and each of its 11 floors were designed by one of 19 different architects. This five-star hotel has a spa, a gym, a swimming pool, a gourmet restaurant and 34 deluxe suites. The idea behind the project was to give guests a wide variety of experiences — with the help of avant-garde architecture, unusual lighting and the use of innovative materials.

Hotel Puerta América
PRICE: **FROM $290 TO $2,175 A NIGHT**
Information: **http://www.hoteles-silken.com/HPAM**

The Literary Layover

When you reserve a room at the Library Hotel in New York don't forget to tell them what you like to read. Each of the hotel's 10 floors corresponds to one category of the Dewey decimal system: social sciences, languages, literature, history, etc. Every room has about a hundred works on a specific theme related to the floor's category. So if you opt for the seventh floor, dedicated to the arts, you can choose among six rooms whose private libraries — and decoration — focus on architecture, painting, music, photography, fashion or the performing arts.

Did you know?

The Library Hotel prides itself on having the largest private collection of rare books in New York.

Library Hotel
PRICE: **$450 A NIGHT**
Information: **http://www.libraryhotel.com**

Staying after Class

At a school like this you won't mind detention. You can scribble on the chalkboard in your room or head down to the auditorium to see what's playing — or you can have a drink at one of the bars. The Kennedy School in Portland, Oregon, has been turned into a hotel. This former elementary school has kept much of its scholastic charm, but today there are no rules against chewing gum, running in the corridors or falling asleep in class. And the level of sophistication is just a little bit higher: there are movies and concerts in the old auditorium and artwork in the hallways, and the hotel keeps its guests informed about cultural events in the area.

Kennedy School
PRICE: **FROM $99 TO $130 A NIGHT**
Information: **http://www.kennedyschool.com**

The Red Hotel

Take advantage on your next trip to Germany to immerse yourself in history. The Ostel GDR-Design-Hostel in Berlin will help you. It offers a journey through time, back to the days when Germany was split in two and the Berlin Wall ran through the middle of the city. Appealing to a sense of both irony and nostalgia, the Ostel cultivates its East German heritage. The personality cult of the German Democratic Republic is recalled with numerous portraits of former president Honecker, and the walls of the hotel are covered with brightly colored geometric designs in pure 1960s style. There's Formica everywhere, and wireless technology is, well, nonexistent.

Did you know?

"Ostalgie" — or nostalgia for the former East Germany — has become a veritable business. Older Germans are happy to find reminders of a world that was swept away so quickly, and younger people, often unable to find work, are attracted to the idealism — however false — of "the good old days."

Ostel
PRICE: **FROM $13 TO $42 A NIGHT**
Information: **http://www.ostel.eu**

An Ocean Runs through It

The Radisson SAS hotel in Berlin offers its best customers rooms with a view... of the aquarium. Since 2003 the Radisson is the happy owner of the largest cylindrical aquarium in the world: over 80 feet (24 m) tall, 36 feet (11 m) in diameter and with 1,800 cubic yards (1,376 sq. m) of saltwater. The aquarium and its 2,600 "guests" have their own staff of divers to prepare their meals and keep the place clean. The Aquadom's wall's are made of high-resistant acrylic glass, and a transparent elevator goes up through the center of the cylinder, giving human guests a close look at the 56 species of fish in the aquarium.

Radisson SAS Berlin
PRICE: **$377 A NIGHT FOR A ROOM WITH A VIEW**
Information: **http://www.berlin.radissonsas.com**

Dubaï
the New El Dorado

With its forest of 600 skyscrapers, its 300 hotels and the largest shopping mall in the world, Dubai has become not just a major center of international trade, but the uncontested kingdom of everything that's over the top.

Yet, just 40 years ago, Dubai was a small fishing port languishing under the desert sun. It all started in 1969 with the discovery of oil. But very quickly the reigning Al Maktoum family understood that the region could not rely forever on this valuable resource, which experts estimate will run out in 2020. So they began planning for a post-oil economy.

Starry, Starry Night

Towering over 1,000 feet (305 m) into the sky, the Burj Al Arab Hotel is one of the tallest palaces in the world — it's also the only seven-star hotel on the planet. Shaped like a billowing sail, this architectural marvel was built on an artificial island, which includes a private beach. It's the ultimate in luxury and priced at between $1,000 and over $18,000 a night.

Burj Al Arab
http://www.burj-al-arab.com

Reaching for the Sky

Burj Dubai,
or the Dubai Tower,
is still under construction,
but it already holds the
title of the world's tallest
skyscraper. Its final height is
being kept secret, but it'll be
somewhere between 2,600
and 3,000 feet
(792 – 915 m) – about
twice as tall as the Empire
State Building or three
times the height of the
Eiffel Tower. Burj Dubai was
built to be a beacon in the
desert and an icon of the
new Middle East. At its base
will be the largest luxury
shopping mall on earth.

Burj Dubai
http://www.burjdubai.com/

Their idea, which perhaps seemed a bit crazy at the time, was to make Dubai one of the largest tourist destinations in the world. With an army of diggers, graders and dump trucks – and today about 30 percent of the world's cranes – the emirate launched a colossal building project. And in order to encourage investment, there are no limitations on foreign ownership of property. As a result, some of the world's wealthiest people, including many English and Russians, are pouring money into the region.

But Dubai isn't going to stop there. It has plans to attract even more visitors with construction plans that rival those of the pharaohs: the tallest building in the world, a group of artificial islands and, coming soon, Dubailand, the biggest amusement park on the planet, which will make that place in Orlando look like a mom-and-pop operation. Dubailand will have 45 different theme parks, of which the most eagerly anticipated is "Restless Planet," devoted to dinosaurs. Visitors will be able to see about a hundred incredibly realistic animatronics – and these ancient reptiles will be watching your every step.

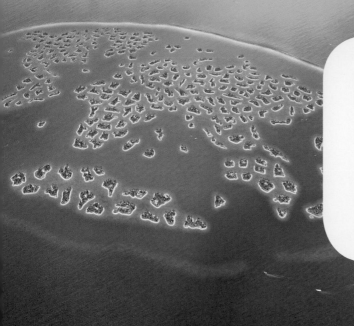

The World in an Archipelago

"The World" project is a group of artificial islands laid out in the shape of the globe. Each island will be developed for different purposes, including residential, resort and commercial uses — all in the middle of a turquoise sea. About half of the islands have already been sold, though construction of the archipelago's infrastructure is just beginning. Celebrities such as Richard Branson and Rod Stewart have purchased islands, whose prices range from about 6 to thirty-six million dollars.

The World
http://www.theworld.ae

Water World

Crescent Hydropolis Resorts is planning a series of oceanic settlements, starting with a luxury underwater hotel in Dubai. Guests will be greeted at a stunning wave-shaped land station on Jumeirah Beach, which will include a high-tech movie theater and marine biology research labs. Then they'll be whisked off on a silent train through a tunnel that leads to the submarine palace. This spacious hotel in the Persian Gulf will include restaurants, bars, a spa, concert hall and ballroom, besides 220 elegant suites — all with an ocean view.

Crescent Hydropolis Resorts
http://www.crescent-hydropolis.com

Joined at the Top

The Palm Trump Tower, like any good luxury hotel in Dubai, will have its own stores, restaurants, fitness center and private beach. But this five-star hotel and residence complex has a unique design: its two towers rise high into the city's skyline before joining near the top and forming a single point.

Trump International Hotel and Tower
http://www.trump.com

The Dubai Dance

Dubai's skyline is getting more sensual, and architect Zaha Hadid's awarding-winning design, which includes three towers, will be one of the reasons why. The middle building will be joined to one of the other towers at the base and will curve over to connect with the third tower at the top in a "fluid choreography." According to the builders, this flowing composition signals a new phase in urban architecture.

Business Bay Signature Towers
http://www.arup.com/gulf

The Butterfly Jungle

Situated less than a quarter mile (0.5 km) off the coast of Dubai, the Apeiron hotel will seem like an isolated haven. The only access will be by yacht or helicopter. But once you're there you'll find a whole range of activities: fine dining or exercising in the gym while enjoying an undersea view, swimming in the lagoon, sunbathing on the artificial beach, taking in a movie or even admiring the works in the art gallery. And the Apeiron will be environmentally friendly; its butterfly-shaped structure will be covered with solar panels that will provide much of the hotel's energy. And while the deluxe suites will be dedicated to the comfort of the guests, the double-height top floor will be reserved for... butterflies. These charming insects will be able to flutter around in a special climate-controlled environment, offering a magical interior atmosphere to match the dramatic view of the Arabian Gulf.

Apeiron
PRICE: **PROJECT STILL IN DEVELOPMENT**
Information: **http://www.sybarite-uk.com/131.htm**

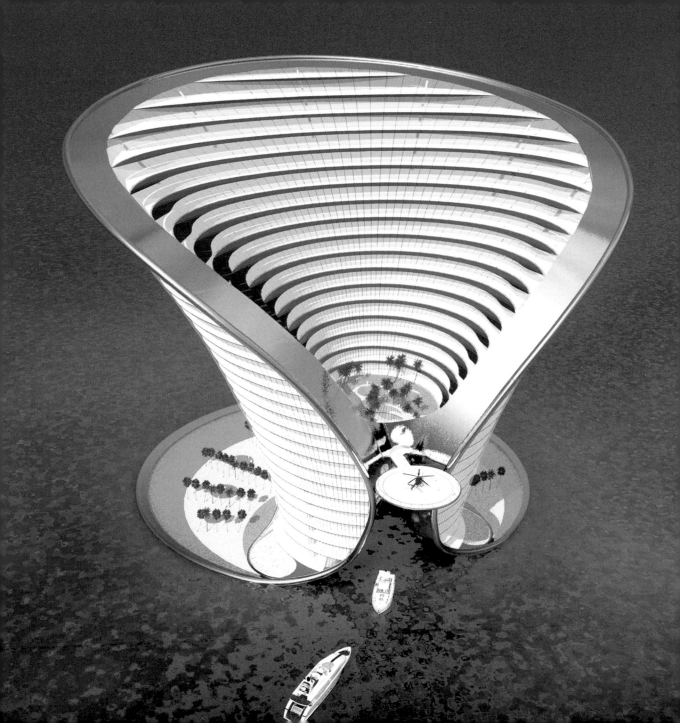

Rooms with an Underwater View

Welcome to your amphibious suite! The architect Giancarlo Zema has dreamed up an incredible idea: a semisubmerged hotel resort in the sea, which looks a bit like a luxurious squid. Inspired by the *Star Wars* world of Gungan City, Amphibious 1000 will combine spectacular views of the sky, the earth and the sea. The complex, which will cover 250,000 square feet (23,255 sq. m), will offer a large array of facilities including meeting rooms, fitness areas, a panoramic restaurant and an interactive museum of marine life. The hotel's floating "jelly-fish" suites will be anchored along platforms, or tentacles, that will reach out into the water. Each, of course, with an underwater view. The project's estimated cost is $500 million.

Amphibious 1000
PRICE: **PROJECT STILL IN DEVELOPMENT**
Information: **http://www.giancarlozema.com/**

The Profoundly Ecological Hotel

An aquatic theme runs throughout the dramatic Songjiang Hotel project in China, which is designed as a modern and ecological place to stay. The hotel will be located in the Songjiang region, noted for its natural beauty. Situated in a water-filled quarry that's over 300 feet (90 m) deep, part of the hotel itself will be underwater. Numerous terraces and cascades will reinforce the feeling of being in an abyss. There is also an aquarium planned, and the site will be surrounded by waterfalls and lakes. The roof of the complex will be covered with plants, and geothermal energy will be used for heating. In summer the naturally low temperature of the quarry will help cool the hotel.

Songjiang Hotel
PRICE: **PROJECT STILL IN DEVELOPMENT**
Information: **http://www.atkinsdesign.com**

Endless Cruise

Spend you life cruising around the world in a unique environment while avoiding import duties and perhaps even income tax. The Freedom Ship will allow you to do just that. And it's going to be enormous. The plans call for a vessel 4,500 feet (1,372 m) long, 750 feet (229 m) wide and 350 feet (107 m) high, rising 25 stories above its main deck. Designed for a population of 100,000, the ship will accommodate 40,000 residents, 30,000 daily visitors, 10,000 overnight hotel guests and 20,000 full-time crew members. This veritable floating city will include schools, a hospital, hotels, restaurants, stores, banks, offices, warehouses, a casino and an airport. Continually circumnavigating the globe, the vessel will stop at major costal cities and exotic ports of call, offering a wide range of commercial opportunities for the onboard businesses and ever-changing tourist attractions for the inhabitants. Estimated cost of the project: about $10 billion.

Freedom Ship
PRICE: **APARTMENTS RANGE FROM $180,000 TO $44,000,000**
Information: **http://www.freedomship.com**

The Home
of Your Dreams

Home, sweet, home... Inside a jellyfish, floating between the surface of the water and the depths of the ocean. Or in a clearing surrounded with strange green towers, where the living room opens up to the outside world. Or in house whose different floors are in harmony with nature and move with the wind. When you live in a constantly changing world, habitats need to evolve as well, bringing variation and surprises to everyday life. Innovative architecture can help make it happen, so that a room of one's own still leaves the door open to that chance meeting — and the dreams of a lifetime.

Drifting through Life

Waking up in the middle of a school of fish, having a sunny breakfast surrounded on all sides by water, that's what life's like in the floating home designed by the architect Giancarlo Zema. The Jelly-fish 45 has five levels, including a panoramic globe situated about 10 feet (3m) underwater. With all the conveniences of more traditional homes, the Jelly-fish 45 includes a kitchen and bathrooms and can accommodate up to eight people.

Jelly-fish 45
http://www.giancarlozema.com

Seoul Commune 2026
http://www.massstudies.com

In the very individualistic Korean society, the Seoul Commune 2026 project is trying to bring together public and private spaces with the help of avant-garde architecture. The mobility of the structure will allow it to adapt to changing trends in society — such as increasing divorce rates and the aging of the population — by offering areas designed for individuals as well as others in which people can meet and socialize.

Contemplation and Wind Shaped Pavilions
http://www.humanshelter.org

With its unusual shape, the Contemplation Pavilion (left) was designed to encourage observation and meditation. The Wind Shaped Pavilion (right) is constructed around a central axis, but each floor will be free to rotate and move independently with the wind. The forms of the houses designed by Michael Jantzen are inspired by the natural world and recall the fragility and constant evolution of living beings.

Dining Down Under

In some public aquariums part of the tour includes a stroll under the sea on a moving sidewalk, but until now no one has thought of stopping along the way to eat. With their new Ithaa restaurant, the Hilton resort on Rangali Island in the Maldives offers fine dining under the water. At about 16 feet (5 m) below the surface, this magical place will make you feel like you're having a meal with Captain Nemo 20,000 leagues under the sea.

Did you know?

This unique eating place is reserved for the happy few. It only seats 12, and children are accepted "at the restaurant's discretion." If you're able to get a reservation, you'll enjoy an unforgettable dining experience with an Indian Ocean coral reef as background. And if meals at the Ithaa — which means "pearl" in the Maldivian language — aren't exactly cheap, it's partly because it cost several million dollars to build this little marvel.

Ithaa Undersea Restaurant
PRICE: **FROM $120 TO $250**
Information: **http://conradmaldivesrangali.com**

Incoming Meals

The S' Baggers restaurant, which opened in the summer of 2007 in Nuremburg, Germany, is the first fully automatic eatery in the world. With a decor suggesting something between a carnival and a flying saucer, it offers a vision of the restaurant of the future. After being greeted at the door you'll never see another employee. Ordering and payment are done at your table using a touch screen, and your food arrives from up in the sky on metal rails that snake through the restaurant like miniature roller coasters. While you're waiting for your meal you can follow its progress on the screen.

Did you know?

The restaurant's kitchen — staffed by living and breathing human chefs — is on the top floor so, with a little help from gravity, meals can spiral down to your table in just a few quick turns.

S' Baggers
PRICE: **TAPAS DISHES FOR $4 TO $15**
Information: **http://www.sbaggers.de/**

The Dark Side of the Restaurant

Opened in Paris in 2004, the bar-restaurant Dans le Noir ("In the Dark") offers an unusual dining experience: a full meal in total darkness. While eating or enjoying a glass of champagne, Dans le Noir allows its guests to experience the world of the blind and at the same time to fully appreciate what's on their plates. Plunged into the world of the sightless, customers are greeted, guided to their tables and served by visually impaired personnel. The restaurant takes advantage of this reversal of roles to offer a menu full of surprises. All potential light sources (cell phones, lighters, watches) are confiscated at the door: if you're going to do this, you have to play by the rules.

Did you know?

Dans le Noir is a small chain that now has restaurants in London, Moscow and Warsaw.

Dans le Noir
PRICE: **FROM $54 TO $62**
Information: **http://www.danslenoir.com**

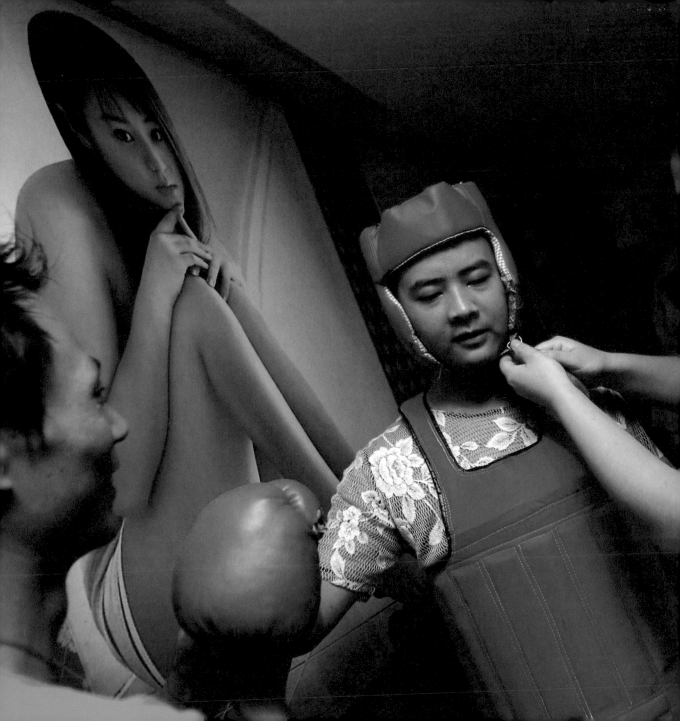

A Smashing Good Restaurant

Modern life is full of stress, especially at work. To relax, what could be better than a nice lunch break. At a new restaurant in Nanjing, China, "break" is the operative word. If the waiter's too slow or the chicken's too dry, just smash the dishes, bust up the furniture or pound away on a sandbag. Best of all, you can describe your worst enemy to the waiter, who will play the part — and let you punch him without ducking or hitting back. For the moment, there's only one of these rather unusual eating establishments that lets you get it all out — but if the stress factor in today's global economy gets any worse, the idea just may catch on.

Did you know?

Getting rid of your stress isn't free: broken plates and bowls will add $1.35 each to your bill and other dishes can cost up to $27 a piece. If you decide to vent your frustrations on the stereo system, you'll be out an additional $135.

The Rising Sun Anger Release Bar
PRICE: **MINIMUM $7**
Information: **http://news.bbc.co.uk/**

"Can I get you a drink — or a transfusion?"

At the Clinic bar and restaurant in Singapore they really look after you. And if you like syringes, hospital beds and all kinds of pills, this place — designed by contemporary British artist Damien Hirst — is definitely for you. Comfortably seated in a wheelchair, you won't be eating insipid hospital food with cold mashed potatoes and a lame piece of ham here. Instead, in this willfully stark but playful atmosphere, you can sip on unique cocktails (like nitro-sangrias, grapefruit and basil mojitos or piña coladas) served in drips, sprays, spoons or lozenges — or enjoy an upscale meal. It's all good fun, but it probably isn't the best place to go the night before a blood test.

Clinic
PRICE: **VARIES DEPENDING ON DRINKS AND FOOD**
Information: **http://www.theclinic.sg**

Pie in the Sky

To get to the restaurant go just above the rooftops and head toward the third cloud on the right. With Dinner in the Sky your eating experience is taken to new heights — 160 feet (49 m), to be precise. First offered in Brussels, these meals on the outer limits allow you to bring together about 20 guests, not counting the sun and the wind. A spectacular view is guaranteed. For those very special occasions, the gastronomical crane can be brought to any location in Europe.

Did you know?

The Belgian company also offers the option of musical accompaniment. For an extra charge, a grand piano and pianist can be suspended from a second crane near your dinner guests.

Dinner in the Sky
PRICE: **APPROXIMATELY $14,125 FOR 20 PEOPLE**
Information: **http://www.dinnerinthesky.com**

Spacing Out

Already more men have walked on the moon than have been to the bottom of the ocean abyss. Space democratization is on the way: Richard Branson, president of the Virgin Group, which now includes Virgin Galactic, is scheduled to launch low-cost space flights in 2008, and the reservation list is already getting long. The Russian Space Agency, which is profiting from these kinds of flights, is booked until 2009. But the moon is only the beginning. There are already plans to go to Mars and beyond, and about 30 or so spaceports, which will offer orbital and suborbital flights, have sprung up around the

Own a Piece of the Moon

If you have a little extra money you don't know what to do with, why not buy some property on the moon? Someday your grandchildren will be able to build their dream house on the land and spend their space vacations there. And with lots starting at just $18.95 an acre, you'd better buy now — before inflation sets in and prices go sky high.

An acre on the moon
http://www.lunarregistry.com

world. Totally separate from official space agencies like NASA, these private spaceports are preparing for the takeoff of tourism in outer space. According the Futron consulting agency, by 2021 the number of space travelers could reach 13,000 a year.

Plans are also underway for luxury accommodations for lunar tourists. Veritable palaces are being designed that will make use of varying levels of gravity to allow guests to experience weightlessness as well as vacation with their feet firmly planted on the ground. And at the bar you'll be able to sip on cocktails with your legs floating out in front of you. But even with falling prices, space tourism will remain a getaway for the rich for some time to come. Poorer dreamers will just have to make do with staying home and launching their genes on a trip in their place. For $50, the Celestis Company will send a sample of your DNA into space. You won't have any photos to show your friends, but you will be able to brag that a little part of you has traveled out into the great unknown.

Celestial Nourishment

How about a nice brick of Neapolitan ice cream extra dry and crunchy. Completely dehydrated, this delightful dessert can keep for years — just in case you get lost in space. And the taste? Well, after you've chewed it for a while and moistened it up with your saliva, it's almost creamy.

Freeze-dried ice cream
http://www.thespaceshop.com

Moon Money

Interplanetary space now has its own money, the QUID. Developed by Travelex in cooperation with a team of scientists at the British National Space Centre and the University of Leicester, the tokens are made of polytetrafluoroethylene (the material used in Teflon) and are lozenge shaped with rounded edges. They can resist changes in pressure and temperature as well as corrosive materials and are unaffected by magnetic fields or cosmic radiation. The current exchange rate is about $12.50 for one QUID.

The QUID
http://www.travelex.com

The Lunatic Fringe

Designed by the architect Hans-Jurgen Rombaut, the Lunatic hotel will be opening its doors in 2050. The hotel, built in the shape of a spaceship, will offer guests unforgettable experiences. The hull of this "sensation machine," as Rombaut calls it, will be reinforced with moon rock to protect visitors and staff from radiation and the extreme temperatures on the moon's surface.

Lunatic
http://www.rombaut.nl

Out of This World

In just a year or two you may be sitting down looking at a friend's vacation pictures taken from about 70 miles (113 km) above the earth. Passengers on this new kind of pleasure cruise will go through a three-day training program, which includes preparation for a zero-gravity experience. They'll also be familiarized with the equipment they'll be using and will have to undergo medical testing. The spaceships will be able to take six passengers and will begin with a weekly schedule, eventually expanding to two flights a day. The first flights should begin sometime in 2008. Welcome to space!

Did you know?

Richard Branson, president of Virgin and Virgin Galactic, once recalled: "I clearly remember that day in 1961, when I was watching live images of two men traveling toward another world. I was spellbound. And I vowed that, one day, I too would go up in space. It's taken longer than I'd imagined... but Virgin Galactic is in the process of becoming the world's first company to offer regularly scheduled flights into space."

Virgin Galactic
PRICE: $200,000 (ONE-WAY TICKETS NOT AVAILABLE)
Information: **http://www.virgingalactic.com**

The Space Hotel

This hotel's got a lot more stars than any other. Robert Bigelow, the project's founder, purchased patents from NASA in order to be able to build the first inflatable hotel in space, and he hasn't hesitated to spend about $500 million already on the venture. Genesis I, a scaled-down model of the final project, was launched on July 12, 2006, and Genesis II went up at the beginning of 2007. The modules are made of a special material that's resistant to space debris and micometeorites that might hit the hotel. The grand opening is scheduled for 2012.

Did you know?

In an ideal orbit just beyond the earth's atmosphere — where the sun rises 15 times a day — the Galactic Suite Space Resort (http://www.galacticsuite.com) will offer a zero-gravity spa.

Genesis
PRICE: **$8,000,000 PER STAY**
Information: **www.bigelowaerospace.com**

Look Out Below

Free-falling 300,000 feet (91,440 m) at 2,500 miles (4,023 km) an hour — now that's an extreme sport. Researchers at the company Orbital Outfitters are actually working on this form of "space diving," which could save astronauts' lives in the case of spacecraft malfunctions. The wife of one of the project's developers, in fact, died in the explosion of the space shuttle Columbia. That's one big jump for a man, one really giant leap for mankind.

Space Diving
PRICE: **PROJECT STILL IN DEVELOPMENT**
Information: **http://orbitaloutfitters.com**

Once You're
Done with This Life

Do you find the idea of a classic coffin a bit boring? Looking for more choices than just deciding what kind of padded lining or wood color you'll have? Horrified at the idea of ending up in an ugly urn on some shelf in the living room? Don't despair — in the 21st century, death is taking on a whole new look. Surprising, shocking and sometimes wildly unconventional, these new ways of dealing with mortality allow you to personalize your last exit from this life and your grand entrance into the next. Coffins, for example, can be customized to reflect the unique character of the deceased. You can get them shaped like

Crazy Coffins

The English have found a way to maintain their famous eccentricity even after their last breath. Vic Fearn & Company makes special-order coffins in all sorts of styles to satisfy their customers' most extravagant dreams. These rather bizarre works of art are crafted to look like a Rolls Royce, a guitar, a ballet shoe or an airplane. An egg-shaped coffin was even created for a woman who wanted to pass into the next world in the fetal position.

Crazy Coffins
http://www.crazycoffins.co.uk

E-mails from Beyond

Sitting around a table in a darkened room at a séance to communicate with the dead is so passé. In the twenty-first century, the dearly departed send messages... by e-mail. A new kind of Internet site allows you to write messages intended for your friends or loved ones that are sent out after you've passed at whatever dates you've chosen. That way you can maintain your former relationships with personal messages, photos and videos sent from beyond the grave. It's never too late to work on your reputation as the perfect friend or relative who always remembers birthdays or other special occasions.

Messavista
http://www.messavista.com

The Undersea World of Granddad

Burial at sea is an old tradition among sailors, but a cemetery under the sea, that's a whole new concept. The Neptune Memorial Reef was inaugurated in November 2007 off the coast of Miami, close to Key Biscayne. At a depth of about 50 feet (15 m), it's a veritable sunken city, with arches, gates, roads, columns and two magnificent lion sculptures. Each monument is designed to accommodate a certain number of funeral urns, with prices varying according to the exact placement chosen. The Neptune Memorial Reef has room for up to 125,000 urns.

Neptune Memorial Reef
http://www.nmreef.com

Ashes to Ashes, Dust to Art

Totally fed up with your mother-in-law? Then get revenge by offering yourself a painting — made out of her ashes. That way you'll be able to admire her beautiful smile every day in the living room, or perhaps the toilet. It's called "Art in Ashes." Mona, a German-born artist, creates original oil paintings that incorporate the ashes of those who have passed away. You can choose an already completed work, to which the artist will add your loved one's remains, or commission a painting to your own specifications.

Most of the works are abstract and come in a variety of sizes and color schemes, so there's something for everyone. Mona works out of her studio in the Texas city of — Corpus Christi. Where else?

Art In Ashes
http://www.artinashes.com

eggs or guitars or even dumpsters. Once you put your mind to it, who knows what you'll come up with? In fact, death seems to be a source of almost unlimited inspiration: transforming your ashes into a diamond or part of an artificial coral reef or a piece of fine porcelain. You can also opt for more spectacular finales, like having your remains explode in the sky in a shower of fireworks or sending them off for a final trip into outer space. And what if there is life after death? Some people have decided to try to stack the deck in their favor by sending out messages after they've passed away or deciding to wait in a deep freeze until a doctor charming wakes them up from their lifeless sleep. Sound like a bunch of anecdotes about the lunatic fringe? These may not be the most common practices in the world, but today more and more people aren't satisfied with trying to create a unique lifestyle — they also want to determine their own style of death.

Into the Heavens

Someday we'll all go to heaven, and why not in a rocket? Memorial Spaceflights offers a unique service to commemorate the end of one's earthly existence. Once the deceased has been cremated, the ashes are placed in a rocket that takes them to their final resting place — somewhere in space (or just for a commemorative ride). Options include a memorial spaceflight with return to Earth, a launch into Earth orbit, a trip to the moon or a flight into deep space.

Did you know?

Celestis has announced that it has made an agreement with Odyssey Moon Limited to send funeral ashes to the moon with the goal of "extending humanity's reach to the stars."

Memorial Spaceflights
PRICE: **FROM $495 TO $12,500**
Information: **http://www.memorialspaceflights.com**

The Ultimate Grand Finale

Do you want to pull off a really spectacular exit? Rather than a regular, old, sad ceremony, why not go out with a bang? Several companies now offer services dispersing funeral ashes in an explosion of fireworks — either as a dramatic ending to a classic ceremony or as the beginning of an entirely new tradition. Only part of your ashes are actually dispersed; the family can keep the rest in an urn. The fireworks display is organized by professional pyrotechnical experts, who of course follow all standard security procedures. All you need to do is choose whether you'd prefer showers of sparks in lightning blue, fiery red or glowing green.

Did you know?

You can opt for a do-it-yourself memorial fireworks display to set off in your own backyard. Or perhaps a short cruise to have your ashes dispersed over the Pacific — with skipper, champagne and hors d'oeuvres provided.

Heavens Above Fireworks
PRICE: **FROM $250**
Information: **http://www.heavensabovefireworks.com**

Grandma in the Sky with Diamonds

According to James Bond, "Diamonds are forever." So why not transform Grandpa or Grandma into family jewels? Thanks to a new procedure developed by a Russian scientist, a Swiss company is now offering synthetic diamonds made out of funeral ashes — a process possible thanks to the carbon contained in the human body. All you need to do is send them about a pound (0.5 kg) of ashes. They're then heated and processed, transforming them into graphite powder. The next step is exposure to extremely high pressure and temperature, during which the raw diamond crystallizes. The result is a unique and eternal gemstone, which is delivered with a certificate of authenticity from the Swiss Institute of Gemology. Once cut and polished, the diamonds can be mounted on rings, necklaces, earrings or even a flower-shaped curio. It would make the perfect gift for that special someone — not Grandma's ring, but Grandma on a ring. How cool is that?

Did you know?

You can choose the size and shape of the diamond but not the color — it'll come out slightly bluish or completely transparent, depending on the person.

Algordonza
PRICE: **FROM $5,440 TO $22,475**
Information: **http://www.algordonza.com**

Cold Comfort

Don't want to end up being eaten by worms or transformed into a pile of ashes? Is immortality more what you had in mind? Then try cryonics. Worldwide, there are currently six companies that offer to preserve the bodies of the recently deceased at extremely low temperatures (below −200°F [−29°C]) until progress in medical science allows them to be brought back to life. Cryonics is a very controversial procedure, but there are already more than 150 people patiently waiting in the freezing cold for their resurrection. And if you're a little low on cash some institutions offer a "neuro" option: only your head is preserved — since it takes up less space, it's cheaper.

Did you know?

The person who's been cryopreserved for the longest time is Dr. James Bedford, whose body was frozen in 1967. The most famous "patient" is baseball player Ted Williams, who died in 2002 at the age of 84.

Cryopreservation
PRICE: **FROM $28,000**
Information: **http://www.cryonics.org** or **http://www.algor.org**

Encapsulate Yourself

Had enough of sad, sordid cemeteries? Here's the first high-tech, mobile version. Designed in Switzerland by the etoy artists' collective, this cemetery uses a capsule to stock all sorts of information about the deceased: photos, videos, audio tracks, DNA samples and ashes. The objective is to create a digital memorial of the person who's passed away. There are up to 50 megabytes of memory available for each individual, and the inhabitants of the land of the living can then consult these interactive portraits for the rest of eternity. To house the capsules, etoy created the Sarcophagus, a shipping container mounted on wheels whose inside is covered with a 17,000-pixel LED screen covering the walls, ceiling and floor, and designed to display the information stored in the capsules.

Did you know?

Always ready for a trip, Timothy Leary, the guru of LSD who died in 1996, was the second person to be "encapsulated."

Mission Eternity
Information: **http://missioneternity.org**

Channeling the Dead

As Andy Warhol famously said, "In the future everyone will be world-famous for 15 minutes." What a visionary that Andy was. Today, thanks to Etos TV, everyone really can get his or her moment, even the dead! Etos TV is the first television channel devoted to the grim reaper. Backed in part by the German Funeral Home Association, the channel will begin airing on Astra satellite television. It's a revolutionary project, the association claims, because "death affects everybody." Indeed. Subjects will include information on life insurance and funeral insurance and documentaries about cemeteries, but the main part of the programming will be devoted to televised obituaries — short films produced by the station in memory of the deceased with the aid of personal mementos and documents supplied by families.

Did you know?

The channel has an initial budget of $14.5 million and plans to begin by broadcasting three hours a day. Soon, however, they hope to be on 24 hours a day, 7 days a week — first in Germany and then throughout Europe.

Etos TV
PRICE: **$2,900 FOR A "POSTMORTEM" MEMORIAL PROGRAM**
Information: **http://www.etostv.de**

crazy
toys

Let's play a little, or a lot, or every day if we can. In the crazy world, you don't run — you roll inside a big ball. And you don't walk — you jump along on springs, which is relatively rare for humans, but totally normal if you happen to be a kangaroo on stilts. But anyone, in fact, can turn into one of those strange creatures. You just have to strap on a pair of high-tech shoes, and to take a little tour of your grounds why not just get the UFO out of the garage?

Playtime isn't just that moment after all your work is done, when you can finally relax. Today it's also a way to make those somewhat too serious or unpleasant tasks a little more fun. Picking up your dog's little treasure so your fellow citizens don't step in it, for example, is just a little more enjoyable if you've got a chic leather wallet specially designed to hold your poop bags. You might also be happier to get up in the morning if it involved a little game of chasing the alarm clock around the room. And as long as we all seem to be regressing back to childhood, we might as well take our pets along with us and get them their own MP3 players and high-fashion wigs. They might not exactly be thrilled to see themselves with blue hair, and they might not particularly like being put in a washing machine, but no one's asking their opinion. Kids can be so cruel sometimes — and it doesn't matter what age they are.

zy toys crazy toys crazy toys crazy
zy toys crazy toys crazy toys craz
zy toys crazy toys crazy toys craz

The Dream of Icarus

Fly like a bird — or even better — like a bat, and take off for the skies at 125 miles (200 km) an hour. Jetman, aka Yves the pilot, soars around the Swiss Alps on his incredible carbon composite wings. In fact, Yves Rossi, a commercial airline pilot and sports enthusiast (who practices paragliding, parachuting and stunt flying) has perfected a pair of jet-powered wings. Humankind's longtime dream of flying freely in the open air was made possible with four small engines attached under these high-tech wings and just enough gas for a short flight. Jetman has already made about thirty flights at a height of over 3,000 feet (915 m), one of which lasted six and a half minutes — making Yves the world's first jet-powered flyer.

Jetman
PRICE: **PROJECT STILL IN DEVELOPMENT**
Information: **http://www.jet-man.com**

Baby You Can Drive My UFO

Make room all you earth cars and all other vehicles stuck to the ground. The M200X "Volantor" is a bit like the Smart Car of flying saucers: small and maneuverable — and this very real craft has already made over 200 successful test flights. Though it can fly up to about 80 feet (24 m) in the air, it's not quite ready for weekend trips. The M200X is designed strictly for personal use. Pack your bags E.T., we're going home!

M200X
PRICE: $90,000; UNITS BUILT AS ORDERED
Information: **http://www.moller.com**

The Motor Copter

With the Personal Air and Land Vehicle (PAL-V), you can take off in your own helicopter without getting off your motorcycle. Its rotor unfolds with the simple push of a button, and off you go. The PAL-V can transport two people, and its aerodynamic design allows it to reach speeds of over 125 miles (200 km) per hour with a range of 375 miles (603 km). However, it is only authorized to take off from airports, and the driver does need a license to fly.

Did you know?

The Transition from Terrafugia (http://www.terrafugia.com), another air and land vehicle, has a cruising speed of 115 miles (185 km) per hour and a range of 460 miles (740 km). Its wings fold up for normal driving.

Personal Air and Land Vehicle
PRICE: **$174,000**
Information: **http://www.pal-v.com**

Bubble Head

How can you explore the exciting undersea world without getting your hair wet? With BOB. This new device allows you to cruise along under the water in a sitting position with your head inside a plastic bubble supplied with air by its own tank. BOB is easy to pilot, with a simple steering mechanism and accelerator pedal. It can go up to two and half knots (almost 3 miles [5 km] per hour) and allows you to stay under for about 50 minutes. This strange little submarine dives or moves toward the surface with the simple push of a button.

BOB (Breath Observation Bubble)
PRICE: **$85 FOR A 2-HOUR RENTAL**
Information: **http://www.bob-diving.com**

Our Yellow Submarine

It's called Goby, and everything about it is cool: lemon yellow color, retro style, panoramic view, sonar, GPS and lots more. And Goby is so compact and easy to maneuver that you don't even need a special license to pilot it. One of its companion models, the Nautilus, created by the same company, was inspired by Jules Verne's *Twenty Thousand Leagues Under the Sea*. But if these cute little crafts that look as though they just floated out of a storybook aren't quite up to your standards, then check out the ultimate in luxury underwater vessels offered by U.S. Submarines in Portland, Oregon (http://www.ussubs.com).

Goby
PRICE: **ABOUT $275,500**
Information: **http://www.palmmarine.ae**

Paintball, Armored Division

Paintball isn't a real war, but the soldiers are on their own. Or are they? With the Funtrak Panzer, a mini paintball tank, things get a little more serious — or silly. This custom-built tank doesn't take up much room in the garage, but it'll definitely improve your game. With a driver's compartment designed for maximum comfort, it fires up to 15 paintballs a second and comes in various colors, ranging from drab olive to blue camouflage, for "ice warrior" operations.

Did you know?

The Funtrak paintball tank was designed by a former member of the British Armed Forces. The vehicle is certified as street legal and thus can be driven on public roads in Britain by a licensed driver.

Funtrak Paintball Panzer
PRICE: **ABOUT $16,000**
Information: **http://www.funtrak.co.uk**

Where the Rich Dolls Live

The last thing you want is your child's doll having to live in some sort of glorified cardboard box. Bespoke Dolls Houses can offer them the possibility of a happy life in a miniature replica of your own home, or you can send them the plans for the house of your dreams. These dollhouses are built with quality materials and are hand painted — they're even wired for electricity. The company take's about a month to build your house. Dollhouses are popular, and several companies specialize in bespoke — or custom-built — models.

Bespoke Dolls Houses
PRICE: FROM ABOUT $1,000 TO $70,000
Information: http://www.bespokedollshouses.com

A Home of Their Own

Whether it's playing lady of the house, nurse, schoolteacher, grocer, firefighter, knight in shining armor or princess, your children's imagination deserves only the best to help it blossom. And with a firestation, mansion or medieval castle just their size, your cute little cherubs will be able to live out their dreams in a world tailor-made for them. Dozens of accessories including refrigerators, mailboxes, pianos, oriental rugs and a bell for the firestation are also available. Some might say that all that makes playtime a bit expensive, but can you put a price on your child's smile?

Did you know?

If deluxe playhouses are over your budget, you can always think about a custom doghouse, but even those are going for about $800 these days.

Lilliput Play Homes
PRICE: **BETWEEN $5,000 AND $9,000**
Information: **http://www.lilliputplayhomes.com**

Your Neighborhood Seen from the Sky

What does your house look like from above? With the Estes Astrovision Video Rocket you don't need a helicopter to find out. This sleek miniature rocket, which can reach a height of 300 feet (90 m), is equipped with a camera that can take three photos or a 12-second video. Once the rocket returns to earth you can download its precious information onto your computer using a USB cable. Hopefully it won't land on your neighbor's head, but at least the camera is impact-resistant.

Estes Astrovision Video Rocket
PRICE: **ABOUT $60**
Information: **http://www.apogeerockets.com**

What's the Buzz?

Who wants to play with an airplane or helicopter when you can have a radio-controlled dragonfly? WowWee is the maker of what it claims to be the first wing-beating remote-controlled insect ever marketed. This cybernetic dragonfly can take off, climb, dive, turn, hover or land with precision. Its stability is assured by a small propeller on the tail, like on a helicopter. The accuracy with which it can be flown makes this toy usable both outside and inside — though you may want to practice a bit before trying it out in Aunt Ester's living room. Its batteries can be charged using the remote control, which means that there's no end to the flying fun. Even darkness won't slow down this bug since its eyes are equipped with LEDs that blink, pulse or shine constantly, depending on its status.

Did you know?

The incredible efficency of the Dragonfly's flight is directly inspired by the movment of birds. When they beat their wings they instinctively create lift, which allows them to fly.

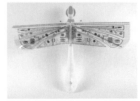

Dragonfly
PRICE: **ABOUT $60**
Information: **http://flytechonline.com**

Taking Giant Steps

Boing! Boing! This is much better than bouncing off the walls. When you strap on a pair of Powerisers it's like turning into a kangaroo or some strange kind of heron or crane. This futuristic footwear gives you instant superpowers. You won't be able to leap tall buildings in a single bound, but you will be able to jump 6 feet (1.8 m) in the air, take 12-foot (3.7 m) steps and make every basket you attempt — even if you're only 5 foot 3 (160 cm). Equipped with special springs, this high-tech sports equipment made of aluminum and fiberglass offers extreme sensations and loads of fun. But before you go bouncing off, it is recommended that you put on a helmet and knee- and elbow-protectors. Even with superpowers you can still fall down.

Poweriser
PRICE: **ABOUT $600 FOR THE ADULT MODEL**
Information: **http://www.poweriser.fr/en**

Head over Hills

Go hurtling down a hill inside a giant PVC ball — now that sounds like fun. The Zorb, invented in New Zealand, and now with a franchise in Tennessee, is actually two concentric balls separated by about 2 feet (0.5 m). When it's inflated, the air between the two balls protects you from the ground, and 1,000 shock-absorbing ties insure that the inner ball stays centered inside the larger one. You can Zorb alone or with a friend, and there are two ways to roll. You can be harnessed inside and go tumbling head over heels or remain free and slosh your way downhill with the help of an added bucket of water that lubricates your ride.

Did you know?

Even if it isn't dangerous, the Zorb is considered an extreme sport and can only be practiced at approved locations. That's why you can't buy or rent one — you have to do your rolling under the supervision of an experienced "Zorb Wrangler."

Zorb
PRICE: **STARTING AT $34 PER PERSON PER RIDE**
Information: **http://www.zorb.com**

The Stretch Mini Cooper

What options were missing on the Mini Cooper? How about two more seats, a television, a minibar, a sunroof and, of course, a Jacuzzi for two. It's all there in the custom Mini XXL created by a Los Angeles-based limousine specialist. In tune with nature, this deluxe Mini allows you to sunbathe and feel the breeze while rolling in luxurious comfort. And the Jacuzzi — supported by an extra rear axle — offers powerful water jets that help you relax while speeding to your destination. There nothing very "mini" about this 20-foot (6m)-plus stretch conversion, but it's sure to get you noticed.

Mini Cooper XXL
PRICE: **NOT FOR SALE**
Information: **http://www.mini.com**

A Massage from Outer Space

If this relaxation capsule looks a little like a spaceship, it shouldn't be surprising. Some of its technology is inspired by research done at NASA. The cocoon-shaped unit offers massages, aromatherapy and audio and video entertainment. The water massage, which uses a unique pulse-jet technology, doesn't get you wet, so there's no need to disrobe. Protected by a special waterproof lining, you just lie back and enjoy while the high-pressure streams of water relax your muscles. In just a few minutes your stress will be gone and you'll feel rested and rejuvenated.

Did you know?

If you want to bring your own music to accompany your massage, the Spacapsule is equipped with a hookup for your Mp3 player.

Spacapsule
PRICE: **ABOUT $25,000**
Information: **http://www.spacapsule.com**

The Sleek Sleep Space

This futuristic oval-shaped structure that looks a bit like a flying saucer is actually a bed — but not just any bed. With a refined minimalist design, the Lomme incorporates the latest technology to create the ultimate sleeping and relaxing environment. An integrated lighting system allows you to choose the color and intensity of the illumination to maximize the benefits of light therapy. It can also simulate sunsets and sunsets to help you drift off to sleep and awaken naturally to the new day. Thanks to an integrated iPod and the protective cocoon with its curved outline, the Lomme allows you to listen to your favorite music without being disturbed by background noise. Luckily the designers had the foresight not to include a refrigerator, because otherwise you'd never want to get out of bed.

Did you know?

On top of all the other features, there's a built-in massage system with a choice of options.

Lomme
PRICE: **ABOUT $63,000**
Information: **http://www.lomme.com**

Clothes
of the future

My stockings make my legs soft and keep them moisturized. My t-shirt is worried about my health and keeps an eye on my temperature. My sweater communicates with the Internet. Today our clothes are taking strange liberties with our bodies. Not content to give us warmth, protection and comfort, they're aspiring to higher goals. Some of them have a made pact with their allies in cosmetics in the form of microcapsules. Invented back in the 1940s and first used for moisturizers and other products, microencapsulation consists in placing certain active ingredients in a type of miniature reservoir. Small amounts of pressure or rubbing or changes in temperature or light intensity cause them to break open and release their contents.

Clothes that Really Take Care of You

"Honey, could you rub some of this cream on me?" You won't have to ask that question anymore because from now on you don't have to rub cream on — you can wear it. When they come in contact with your skin, microcapsules embedded in the fabric of your clothes will slowly release active substances with various cosmetic effects. You can choose from formulas with slimming, moisturizing or antifatigue effects.
Cosmetotextile
http://www.lytess.com

Wearing Your Heart on Your Neck

You don't need to be a poet to express your love to that special someone — even if you're the shy type, your feelings can be as plain as day. And you won't need some sort of life coach to do it. You just need to wear the right jewelry. This new form of body adornment sticks to your skin and will interpret your emotions and display them for all to see. One look at your necklace will let everyone know whether you're as cool as a cucumber or ready to have a nervous breakdown. And Philips has also developed an electronic tattoo that changes color when caressed...

Skintile Electronic Sensing Jewelry
http://www.design.philips.com/probes/projects

Incorporated into various fabrics, these magic little capsules will start working at just the right moment. Are you getting hot and beginning to perspire? Your t-shirt will react immediately, providing you with a sweet-smelling deodorant. Are your legs getting tired and achy at the end of the day? Don't worry, your tights, triggered by the movement of your muscles, will give you a light massage and apply special compounds to stimulate the circulation in your veins. You've never had it so good.

Researchers are also working on products that go beyond just pampering. If a sweater can help keep your skin nice and smooth, it can also protect you from bacteria and germs. The new trend is toward "intelligent biomedical clothing" — a nanny of sorts for all the fragile beings of the modern world, from children to senior citizens to athletes who just don't know when to slow down.

For products such as these, it isn't capsules that make the difference but sensors. Incorporated into the clothing, they constantly transmit information to friends, family members or hospital staff using Bluetooth or other communication technology. Researchers in Singapore, for example, are working on a "granny sitter" blouse whose sensors can detect if a person falls down and immediately inform the family. And then there's a new type of underwear designed to stimulate the muscles of victims of cerebral hemorrhages. When muscle movement is detected, signals are sent to a network of electrodes. Depending on the information received, the electrodes can release a gel incorporated into the garment, which stimulates the person's muscles. It'll also be possible to remotely monitor the vital signs of a patient, which will alert emergency services if a problem occurs. Indispensable? Perhaps. But it's hard to know where all of this is going to take our wardrobes.

A Bootee to Watch over Baby

Newborn babies are fragile things. Modern medicine has developed equipment to monitor their vital signs, but all those wires make that all-important skin-to-skin contact between parents and their babies a bit difficult. To solve that problem French researchers have developed a baby bootee equipped with sensors that keep a constant check on the temperature, heart rate and blood-oxygen level of infants. Any anomalies are immediately signaled on a remote monitoring device, alerting hospital staff or parents.

BBA bootee
http://www.tamtelesante.com

Remote Hugging

Thanks to the Internet we can all see and hear friends no matter where they are in the world. In an attempt to take wireless communication to the next level, scientists in Singapore are working on a method of using the web to transmit touch. For the moment "cyberaffection" research is focused on developing a special type of clothing controlled by a remote computer. A parent will be able to touch a special doll — or "hugging interface device" — and thousands of miles away "Internet pajamas" will reproduce the sensations using pressure and heat elements, simulating a real cuddle — or maybe a good spanking.

ipyjama
http://lpajama.wikidot.com

Let There Be Fashion

You can become a light! Or almost. In any case, with an illuminated dress you'll feel like a star. Made of a combination of optical fibers and traditional material, this special fabric, hooked up to a miniature electric module, lights up with the flick of a switch. Besides clothes it can also be used in purses and even decorative items for the home. Since it's powered by low-voltage batteries there's no danger to the wearer — besides being the center of attention all evening.

Did you know?

The special fiber-optic fabric is washable but can only be folded parallel to the optical fibers in order not to damage them. Five different colors of light are available.

Lumigram
PRICE: **FROM $144 (PURSE) TO $1,014 (LARGE TABLECLOTH)**
Information: http://www.lumigram.com

Can I Put That in a Bra for You?

Triumph brand lingerie is coming to the rescue of Japanese ecologists. In order to reduce the number of plastic bags used in the country — currently about 30 billion per year — they've developed the "Rangers" bra, which transforms into a shopping bag. Made out of recyclable materials, it comes with a matching pair of panties marked with the exclamation, "No!" (and a short message in Japanese to clarify that the "no" refers to plastic bags). A German company has come up with another environmentally friendly concept: to decrease the use of disposable chopsticks used in Asian restaurants they're selling underwear that incorporates reusable ones — that you can whip out at a moment's notice.

Bra Rangers
PRICE: **PRODUCT STILL IN DEVELOPMENT**
Information: **http://www.triumph.com**

Change Your Shoes with a Click of the Heels

The sight of thousands of women on the streets of New York wearing pantsuits and sneakers inspired David Handel to find a way to help them avoid changing their shoes twice a day. Camileon Heels shoes are equipped with retractable heels that allow you to switch from a 3¼-inch (9.5 cm) to a 1½-inch (4 cm) heel in just three easy clicks. There are 14 models currently available, all in relatively classic styles suitable for the workplace. Finally no more lugging around an extra pair shoes or spraining your ankle while running for the bus.

Did you know?

The mechanism used in Camileon Heels shoes was inspired by the designer's son's Transformer toys.

Camileon Heels
PRICE: **ABOUT $435**
Information: **http://www.camileonheels.com**

Slippers with Headlights

In the middle of a sleepy night the bedroom can be a dangerous obstacle course, but turning on the lights can hurt your eyes. These lighted slippers have soft bluish LED headlights that illuminate an area up to about 20 feet (6 m) in front of you and help guide you to the phone, fridge or bathroom. During the day special light sensors prevent the LEDs from coming on needlessly. Brightfeet Slippers run on lithium batteries.

Did you know?

Doug Vick, creator of Brightfeet Slippers, has extensive experience as an inventor, notably in the field of air fresheners and deodorizers. He came up with a fragrant paint additive called Paint Pourri and a spray for trashcans called Fresh Can.

Brightfeet Slippers
PRICE: **ABOUT $58**
Information: **http://www.brightfeetslippers.com**

Sandals You'll Get Attached to

Ah, the pleasures of going barefoot! Communing with nature — or just reducing the back pain caused by that perverse invention, high heels. But on hard or rocky surfaces, or to avoid that ever-lurking shard of glass or present from Fido, what can you do? Go topless! With no straps, the new Topless Sandals give you the great feeling of walking barefoot without having to worry about what you might step on. They literally stick to your feet but don't leave any nasty residue when you take them off — and the "stick" is guaranteed to last a year. With models for both men and women they come in all sizes and a wide variety of colors and designs. So say goodbye to tan lines on your beautiful feet and go topless.

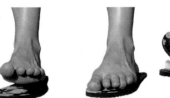
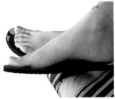

Topless Sandals
PRICE: **ABOUT $12**
Information: **http://www.topless-sandal.com**

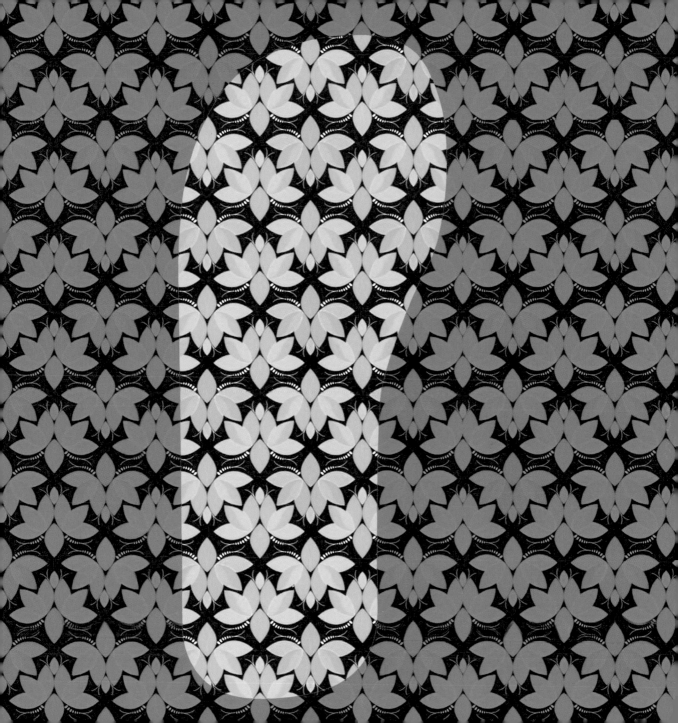

Color Down Under

Ah, a true blond. Or a true blue... With Betty hair colors you can coordinate the hair on the top of your head with your curls in that more intimate region, or what the company refers to as your "hair down there." They've got a wide variety of colors: blond, brunette or, if you're really looking to brighten things up, hot pink "Fun" or blue "Malibu." The basic idea is the same as any other hair dye. First you mix the lightening cream with a spatula and then apply it. After that you put on the coloring itself, allowing it to set for about 20 minutes. And there you have it! Hair down there — to match your hair up top or your eyes or your mood.

Did you know?

Betty also offers stencils to help you create a secret little design in the shape of a star or a heart or even a peace sign.

Betty
PRICE: **ABOUT $20**
Information: **http://www.bettybeauty.com**

A Belly Full of Art

Your baby's on the way, and you're proud of your nice round belly. Baby Art has come up with a method of immortalizing your pregnancy — a condition that, of course, won't last forever. Totally safe for both mother and child, the kit helps you create a unique sculpture of your big belly using a synthetic plaster that can be spread over your entire front, from waist to neck, and dries in about half an hour. The kit comes with a pair of protective gloves, the special plaster and a bottle of oil to protect the mother's skin. Once the plaster is dry you can personalize it with paint or other decorations, an activity the whole family can join in on. After that the only challenge is to figure out what to do with it.

Baby Art Belly Kit
PRICE: **ABOUT $32**
Information: **http://www.babyart.be**

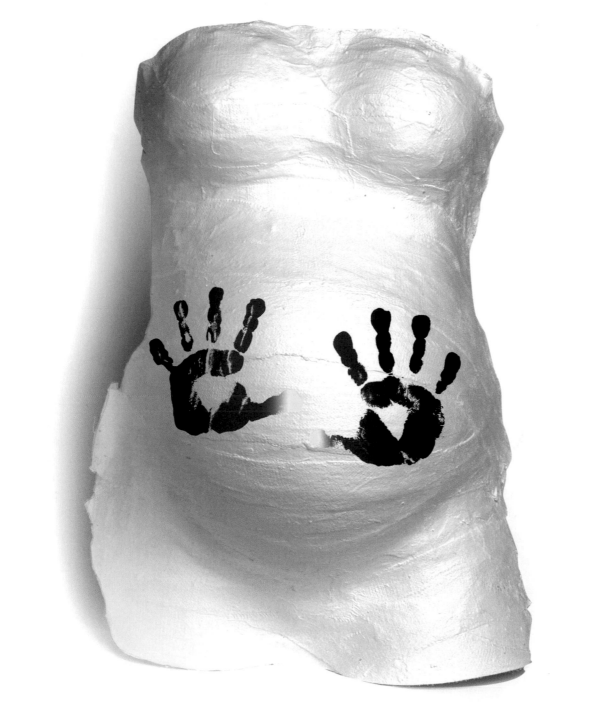

Dressed to Drink

It's not because you're an alcoholic that you can't be practical. And since imbibing a bit too often can leave you with a spare tire, why not speed up the process with a fake belly that doubles as a secret beer or wine reservoir? Not that you couldn't use this handy accessory for coffee or hot chocolate. This removable belly, which will give you the sagging bulge of a veteran beer drinker, is actually a sort of canteen you wear under your clothes. Soft but solid, the Beerbelly is made out of polyurethane and neoprene and can hold 80 ounces (2.4 L) of your favorite drink. To quench your thirst or warm yourself up, just take a discreet sip on the plastic hose that reaches all the way to your mouth. And one undeniable advantage of this system is that the more your drink the smaller your (fake) belly gets.

Did you know?

The company has developed a sexier model designed just for women. The Winerack is a bra that can be filled with your favorite beverage.

The Beerbelly
PRICE: **ABOUT $50**
Information: **http://www.thebeerbelly.com**

My Greatest Hero is Me!

Love, love me, do! If you think of yourself as your own greatest hero — enough to want to see yourself show off your own little hard plastic GI Joe muscles — then check out Hero Builders. Working from photos you send in and your choice of custom clothing, the company will create a 12-inch (30.5 cm) action figure that looks just like you. What a pleasure it'll be to be admired the way you've always deserved. My greatest hero is me!

Hero Builders
PRICE: **ABOUT $425**
Information: **http://www.herobuilders.com**

USB
Portal to Another World

In just a few years the simple USB portal on your computer has become the place to plug it all in. It's so versatile that it can be used to hook up virtually anything and everything. It all started with practical devices for your computer, moved on to gadgets that were more cool than really necessary and has gone totally burlesque. The secret is the fact that this high-speed information link is also a power source. All sorts of cute peripherals can sink their sharp little jacks into the computer and suck out a bit of energy. The most common device is the USB flash drive, a sort of portable information warehouse,

which has become a widely used solution for storing and transporting digital information. About the size and shape of a flat finger, this now indispensable accessory can be personalized in almost any way imaginable. It wasn't long before it was available with cases made out of exotic wood, crystal or gold and diamonds — and came in the shape of dogs, dolls or Mickey Mouse. The Japanese company Solid Alliance (see samples on the page to the right) specializes in unusual — not to say weird — flash drives, that look like rubber ducks, sushi or even breaded shrimp. There's even a pious version in the form of a miniature wooden cross. But the USB flash drive is just the tip of the iceberg. The next thing we knew the USB portal was being used to plug in cup warmers, paper shredders, mini-refrigerators, virtual aquariums, fans, perfume diffusers and plastic desktop rocket launchers. With just a small flat plug you can link up to the whole cyberworld, but what comes back out is a reflection of our fantasies — the part of our digitalized selves that just can't be repressed.

ホワイト

ブラック

(注)実際はこげ茶です

Where's the Alarm Clock?

Clocky looks charming, but its personality is a bit perverse. With a character like a misbehaving pet, this alarm clock won't let you wake up peacefully. It'll let you snooze once, but if you don't get up after that it takes off and rolls around your room looking for a place to hide. The only thing you can do then is get out of bed, find the little devil and muzzle it. The inventor of Clocky, Gauri Nanda, a graduate of MIT, says: "Having an alarm clock hide from me was the most obvious way I could think of to get out of bed. It's a bit ugly, but its unconventional looks keep the user calm and inspire laughter at one of the most hated times of the day."

Clocky
PRICE: **ABOUT $73**
Information: **http://www.nandahome.com**

Where are you, keys?

"What have I done with my keys... and my glasses... and my kid?" The Loc8tor is the faithful friend of the scatterbrained. Equipped with a remote control and several different-colored homing tags, it'll help you find things that you've misplaced or — like your dog or child — that have wandered away. You just have to attach one of the tags to anything that has the annoying tendency to disappear. When the device is activated it'll lead you to whatever you've lost, as long as it's within a radius of 600 feet (183 m).

Did you know?

The Loc8tor's small screen guides you to the lost item showing you the direction of its location.
It can also emit beeps that get louder as you get closer to what you're looking for.

Loc8tor
PRICE: **$199 EACH**
Information: **http://www.loc8tor.com**

Did You Hear Something?

It's looks pretty much like any other loudspeaker, but it could mean the end of family arguments and angry neighbors. The sound emitted by the Audiobeam can't be heard by someone who isn't directly in its path, but if you're in just the right place you'll start to hear voices — though they won't be celestial. Anyone standing beside or behind the speaker doesn't hear a thing. The Audiobeam uses an ultrasonic carrier frequency to send out a signal that only becomes audible when, due to the nonlinearity of air, it becomes demodulated at a certain distance from the speaker. The result is that the sound seems to come out of thin air.

Did you know?

The makers of the Audiobeam hope to market it for exhibitions or theme parks, where various explanations could be given to a visitor without bothering anyone else. Other potential applications include automatic machines with voice functions, which could only be heard by the customer using them.

Audiobeam
PRICE: **ABOUT $4,350**
Information: **http://www.sennheiser.com**

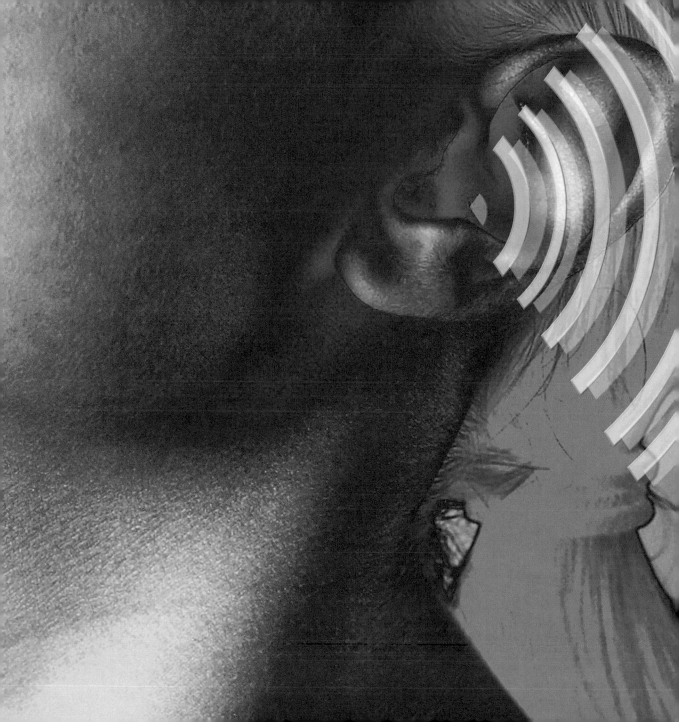

Fruity Water

It's finally here, flavored water right out of the faucet. It comes in grape, lemon, strawberry, peach or raspberry. The Pur Water company offers a faucet-mounted filter that not only removes lead, chlorine and other nasty contaminants from your water but can also add delicious fruit flavors. You just have to slip a cartridge into the specially designed faucet to turn it into a drink dispenser. All the flavors are sugar-free and have absolutely no calories. They do, however, include sweeteners and a nice variety of acids (citric, benzoic, sorbic). But with just one cartridge providing up to 75 servings, any minor drawbacks are just a drop in the bucket — or the kitchen sink.

Pur Water Filtration System
PRICE: **$10 FOR TWO CARTRIDGES; $49 FOR THE FAUCET FILTER**
Information: **http://www.purwater.com**

On-Demand Cocktails

It might not be the Fountain of Youth, but it is a miracle. With a Wi-Fi hookup to a site that allows it to download new recipes, this little wonder can make any cocktail you want. Equipped with a high-quality water filter and automatic sanitizing system, MyFountain is capable of dispensing up to 16 different drinks that always taste fresh. And if you're worried about the random lush hanging around the office — or your home — this automatic bartender includes password protection and the possibility of limiting the amount of any drink dispensed to each user. (It can also control the amount of sugar in each drink for those on a diet.)

Did you know?

You can hook up a keyboard to the fountain and turn it into a fully functioning PC.

MyFountain
PRICE: **STARTING AT $4,000**
Information: **http://digitalbeverages.com/myfountain.htm**

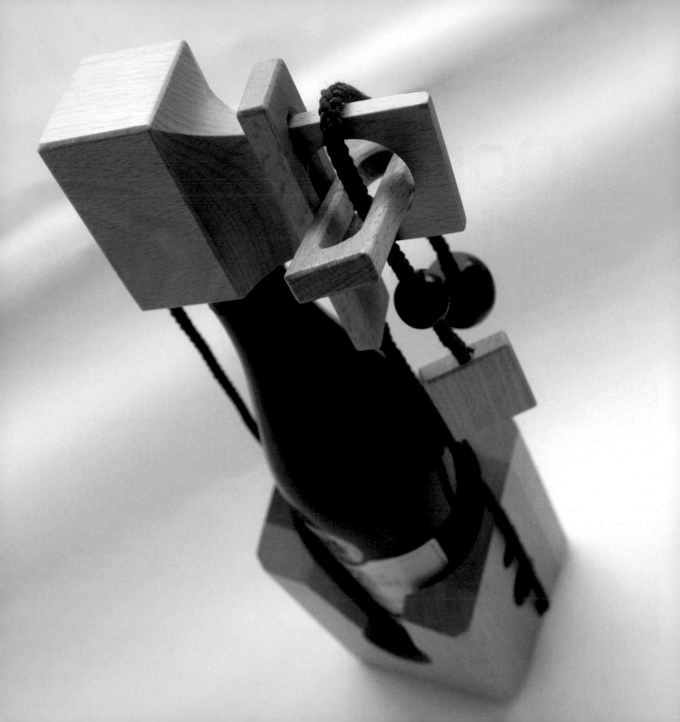

Don't Break the Bottle

Bringing a good bottle of wine along when you're invited to dinner is always a good idea. But with Don't Break the Bottle your host has to earn it. Just place any bottle of your choice (it also works with herb vinegar, olive oil or pretty much any bottle of about the same size) into this wooden puzzle. Too simple? Think again. As all the guests offer their more-or-less helpful suggestions, Don't Break the Bottle ensures that opening the present is almost as enjoyable as drinking it. This brainteaser is reusable, unless, of course, frustration — or thirst — leads to smashing it to bits. Once the puzzle is solved your host will no doubt enjoy the wine you've brought all the more. If everyone ends up stumped, however, you can show off your own genius by releasing the bottle from its wooden shackles.

Don't Break the Bottle
PRICE: **ABOUT $25**
Information: **http://www.seriouspuzzles.com**

Spoiling
Our Best Friends

He gets his clothes from the top designers. He nonchalantly snacks on hors d'oeuvres after his daily workout at the gym. He reveals his innermost troubles to his psychologist then heads off to the hairdresser for a new look before going home to his all-organic dinner. At the end of his life he'll be buried, or perhaps cremated, and given a dignified ceremony. It's a dog's life. Or a cat's. How in the world did we get to buying our pets Vivienne Westwood wardrobes or paying more attention to their meals than a cook at a gourmet restaurant? Lost in a world where friends and lovers seem to come and go with each new season,

Dog Shopping

After having organized a fashion show for pets, upscale retailer Harrods has opened a new section of its department store specializing in jewelry and other deluxe accessories for cats and dogs. A few well-known designers are participating in this lucrative operation to insure that Fluffy and Fido attract as much attention as the rich and famous at their next big soiree. From perfumes to luxurious coats to fine jewelery, this is the place for the most demanding pet lovers.

Harrods
http://www.harrods.com

The Cat's Meow

Offer you cat the role of its life with these magnificent wigs specially designed for it. You have a choice of pink passion, bashful blond, silver fox or electric blue. And if Kitty tries to scratch your eye out for making it look so ridiculous, just tell it that 20% of the profits are donated to the American SPCA.

Kitty Wigs
http://kittywigs.com

Workin' at the Pet-Wash

Everyone knows that you're not supposed to put dogs or cats in the washing machine, but with Lavakan, now you can. This new contraption is like a carwash for pets. It gets them all cleaned up without you having to get anywhere near the bathtub. Once inside the chamber, the machine takes over, putting your pooch or kitty through wash, rinse and dry cycles. In a little less than half an hour they come out fresh and clean — without any of that "wet pet" smell.

Lavakan
http://www.lavakan.cat

Come on Boy, into the Oxygen Chamber

No more fretting over the next birthday gift for your favorite pooch. To restore his energy and make him feel young again, pamper Spot with a really special treatment: the AirPress Company has developed an oxygen therapy chamber adapted for dogs. Just like the ones for humans, It promises to reduce wrinkles, sooth migraines and stimulate weight loss. It'll prove to him that you really love him. What it'll prove to your friends is another story.

Dogs 02
http://www.gadgetbb.com

some people have decided that the only really stable relationship they have is with their pet. Dogs and cats don't just stick around — they provide a friendly presence, moral support and love. Once you get used to considering them as precious companions they start to seem like people, or at least like a part of you. You feel a little more self-assured — and safe — with a powerful animal on the end of a leash, or reflecting your taste with a purebred cat that looks like a sleek sculpture. And what's going to happen to the planet's wildlife when about 8,000 species are endangered? In some cases, they adapt, popping up when you least expect it, right in the middle of modern life and making humans adapt to them. In Canada a brochure entitled *Bears and People* explains what to do if you have an unexpected meeting with a real-life teddy: don't run, speak softly to him, give him space... and don't try and see if he'd look good with your Christian Dior barrette clipped in his fur.

Doing Business with Elegance

When Rex has gotta go, he's gotta go — and as a good citizen you know what your duty is. Pick up the little treasure he's left with the aid of a plastic bag, seal it up and drop it in the nearest garbage can. You can make this whole business just a little more stylish with the Pooch.I poo Bag, a leather wallet designed to hold up to 10 poop bags. Just make sure you don't get it mixed up with your regular wallet.

Pooch.I poo bag
http://www.rockettstgeorge.co.uk

Brightening Up the Dog Days

Dogs with sullen faces or drooping chops will gain a whole new look with this rubber toy. With its hilariously large lips, the Doggy Smile Fetch Toy gives dogs a radiant and happy grin. This toy — so silly that it soon becomes indispensable — is ideal for family reunions, a walk in the park or that special photo for your album.

Doggy Smile Fetch
http://www.iwantoneofthose.com

Sad

Happy

Fustrated

On Guard/
Territorial

Assertive/
Showing off

Your dog is *Needy*.

Hello, Fido?

Is your dog always wandering off? Does it have a total lack of respect for dinnertime? Then get it a cell phone. The PetsCELL clips on to your dog's collar and is waterproof and shock resistant. If it decides to go on an expedition beyond the limit you've programmed into the device, you get a call on your cell phone. You can then locate your pooch with the built-in GPS system. If someone finds your lost dog, they can let you know where it is simply by pushing the "call owner" button and talking to you on the PetsCELL.

PetsCELL
http://www.petsmobility.com

The Translator for Dogs

Japanese dog owners are snapping up Bowlingual translators like hotcakes. This miraculous device records your dog's barking and then classifies the "message" according to six emotional categories with, according to the company, 90 percent accuracy. A microphone transmits the sounds to a portable decoder, which analyzes and displays the results on a small screen. The translator has a repertoire of 200 phrases that reflect what your dog is thinking, such as "I'm sad" or "I want to play" or even "Keep your paws to yourself!"

Bowlingual
http://www.takaratoys.co.jp/bowlingual

Barking to the Beat

The JooZoo is just what your dog needs to climb the social ladder. When it goes on its walks in the park, it'll impress all its friends with this exclusive canine MP3 player — in the form of an 18-carat gold heart-shaped necklace decorated with diamonds! With all its four-footed peers eyeing it with envy, it'll be the cat's meow. The Korean company that makes this indispensable product claims that the Mp3 player's music will reduce your dog's stress and stimulate healthy physical activity. It's especially recommended for when your pet is home alone, to keep it calm, lessen boredom and help avoid depression. It should be noted, however, that during adolescence, even at feeding time, Fido might refuse to take it off, totally ignoring any pleading on your part.

JooZoo
PRICE: **ABOUT $2,000**
Information: **http://www.joozoo.net**

Doga

A h, the relaxing effects of yoga! The silence, the intense concentration... and all that whimpering and barking. In fact, your dog possesses a rich — but hidden — inner spirit, but it may need some help in getting better in touch with it. You can show it how by introducing it to the cobra position and teaching it the benefits of learning to control its breathing in order to dissipate the nervous tension of our modern dog-eat-dog world. Or at least that's what proponents of the new practice of "doga," or "ruff yoga," currently in vogue in the United States, would like you to believe. Dogs and their owners meditate and practice yoga poses together on the same mat (or doggie blanket). During each session, which lasts about 30 to 40 minutes, they share each other's energy and get in touch with their inner selves. And if you both end up with less stress, then why not?

Doga
PRICE: **AVAILABLE ON REQUEST**
Information: **http://www.crunch.com/crunch**

Dancing with the Dogs

According to many specialists, classic methods of obedience training are on the way out. More playful and relaxed techniques that keep man's best friend interested and stimulated are now in vogue. With that in mind, several trainers are offering dance classes to help dogs move in harmony with their masters. They learn to turn, run between their owners' legs, weave back and forth, walk on their hind legs and move backward — all in time to music. It's training that's actually fun for the animal, who of course gets a treat for each correct maneuver. And both dogs and owners are happier.

Canine Freestyle Federation Inc.
PRICE: **AVAILABLE UPON REQUEST**
Information: **http://www.canine-freestyle.org**

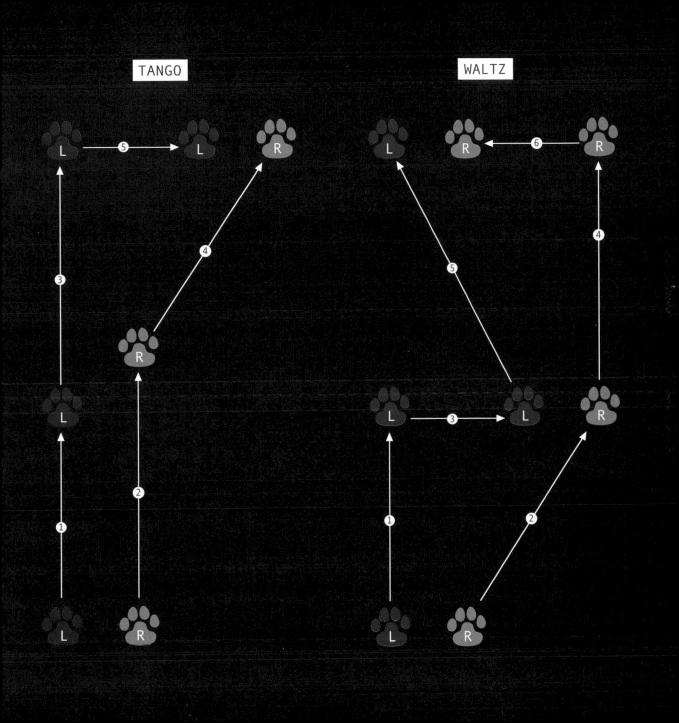

Dogllywood

Do you know the canine stars of Dogllywood? They've all come together in an absolutely magnificent DVD that will captivate your dog's attention for a full 60 minutes. Your pet will certainly appreciate the high level of acting on display in this cinematic masterpiece — and it may even make it forget that you've abandoned it again for the day. This DVD has more than one trick up its sleeve because you can choose between the original soundtrack and a version with relaxing classical music. Bonus materials include a special track designed to get your puppy used to everyday sounds, like cars, trains and thunderstorms, and a "making of" section that takes you behind the scenes to reveal the mysteries of Dogllywood. You and your dog have just got to have this!

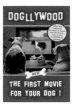

Dogllywood
PRICE: **ABOUT $27**
Information: **http://www.dogllywood.com**

Cat's-Eye View

What in the world does your cat do all day while you're out? Does it wander over to your neighbor's yard hoping to meet that cute feline it hears meowing from time to time or head out to hunt that pesky mouse? If your cat's not talking and curiosity is killing you, then you need the Catcam. Equipped with a 1.3-megapixel digital camera and an SD card slot, it weighs about 2½ ounces (71 g) and snaps pictures at regular intervals throughout the day. The whole thing is housed in a small plastic box attached to your cat's collar. Now you'll know whether Kitty's been unfaithful — purring happily in your neighbor's lap — or just hanging out around the house.

CatCam
PRICE: **ABOUT $65**
Information: **http://www.mr-lee-catcam.de**

Dog Heaven

"For sale: Beautiful colonial-style doghouse in quiet neighborhood. Sunny and comfortable, with parquet floors and cedar siding. Living room, bedroom, playroom and dining area. Central heating and air conditioning. Swimming pool and screened-in porch with exterior lighting fixtures. A must see! You'll love it! From now on you won't be saying, "Get in your doghouse," but "Head back to your palace." Whether it's a classic country-style home, a manor house, a Swiss chalet or some architect's dream, doggie housing has moved to a whole new level. And it doesn't matter that your average pooch would rather be outside rolling around in the mud — or worse. Nowadays it seems that some people see their pets as aspiring to be proud home owners. Dogs haven't yet started inviting over their four-legged friends for a barbecue, but it might not be long. At least Rover can take care of guarding his own house. Beware of (materialistic) dog!

Doggy Dream Homes
PRICE: **VARIES, BUT GENERALLY OUTRAGEOUS**
Information: **http://www.doggydreamhomes.com**

The Doggie Porthole

A window on the world, or at least on the neighbor's backyard. If you can't offer your pet a trip across the country, you can at least satisfy its natural curiosity and enlarge its view beyond the confines of the square patch behind the house. Pet Peek, which can be installed into virtually any wooden fence, gives your dog another point of view. Made of transparent acrylic, this porthole for your dog is 9½ inches (24 cm) in diameter and includes a black trim ring and hardware for attaching it. Now your four-legged friend will be able to keep an eye on the comings and goings of your neighborhood's creatures, both inside and outside its little kingdom. Of course, if it happens to see a fluttering bird or a juicy-looking squirrel just beyond its reach, the window is likely to get a bit steamed up — and it may get a bit frustrated at not being able to leap through the looking glass.

Did you know?

A percentage of the profits from the sales of Pet Peek windows are donated to animal rights associations.

Pet Peek
PRICE: **ABOUT $30**
Information: **http://www.petpeek.info**

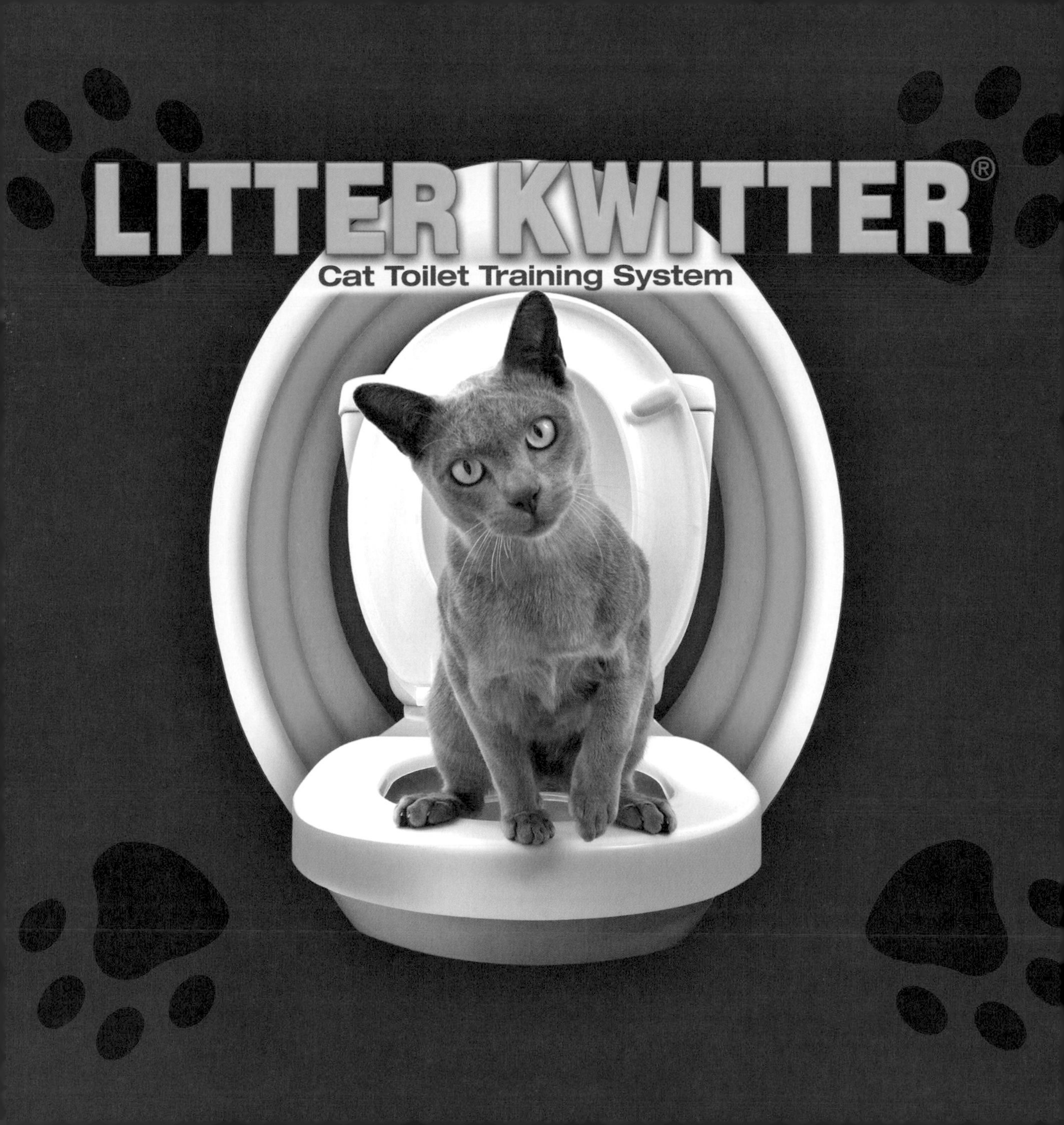
LITTER KWITTER®
Cat Toilet Training System

Kitty Needs to Go to the Bathroom

Your cute little cat is litter trained. Every day it conscientiously scratches around in its litter box, keeping its business out of sight. But if you can't see it, that doesn't necessarily mean you can't smell it. Because even if Kitty is as careful as can be and the litter is scented, you still need to clean out the box regularly. Unless you've got a really modern cat. Then it would use the toilet like the rest of the family. It's possible with Litter Kwitter. In fact, an animal behavior specialist has come up with a training program to teach your cat to use the toilet, employing the same basic approach used in getting babies to move from diapers to a potty to the toilet. With the help of three concentric rings that have increasingly large holes in the middle, little by little you can get your cat accustomed to using a human toilet. In just eight weeks it will have moved from the litter box to the little boys' room. The only thing left is to teach him to flush.

Litter Kwitter
PRICE: **ABOUT $84**
Information: **www.litterkwitter.com**

crazy
ideas

Scientists are incredible! They're basically a bunch of slightly insane nerds let loose in a laboratory.
in some of the most advanced research centers on the planet, from the Massachusetts Institute of Technology (MIT) to design studios in the Netherlands, their hyperactive neurons work on countless projects. These modern wizards have a sense of humor as well as a sense of the public good. Science, in fact, can be quite amusing.
But their bizarre-sounding ideas are actually very serious — helping cure diseases and improve medical treatments or just making our everyday lives easier and more

enjoyable. So why do researchers seem to cultivate this image of being a bit off the wall? No doubt because in order to innovate you have to imagine what hasn't yet been imagined. Why be content with the possible when the real answers lie in what's not possible? Crazy inventors can put a whole room in a box or a telephone in a tooth. They can air condition a brain or turn your hand into a functioning keyboard. They can even transform your morning toast into a message board or make a sticky note sing. Everything's possible. You just have to think of it.

Shooting from the Neck

Are you really excited? Then prove it. The Momenta necklace can detect your inner feelings. In fact more than just a futuristic piece of jewelry, it actually monitors your heart rate. If it increases the Momenta goes into action and begins saving images of whatever event made your heart go wild. That way you'll have a permanent record of "the day you fell in love" or "the day the neighbor's dog scared the heck out of you." And Momenta, actually a full-function PC, is not only able to project your videos on any surface, but it has a touch-gesture interface that allows you to use your programs without hooking up any peripherals. If you're attacked the Momenta will automatically record the scene and then, using a Wi-Fi connection, can immediately send the video to a nearby computer.

Did you know?

The Momenta was one of the entries in the 2007–2008 Next-Gen PC Design Competition sponsored by Microsoft.

Momenta
PRICE: **PRODUCT STILL IN DEVLOPMENT**
Information: **http://www.nextgendesigncomp.com**

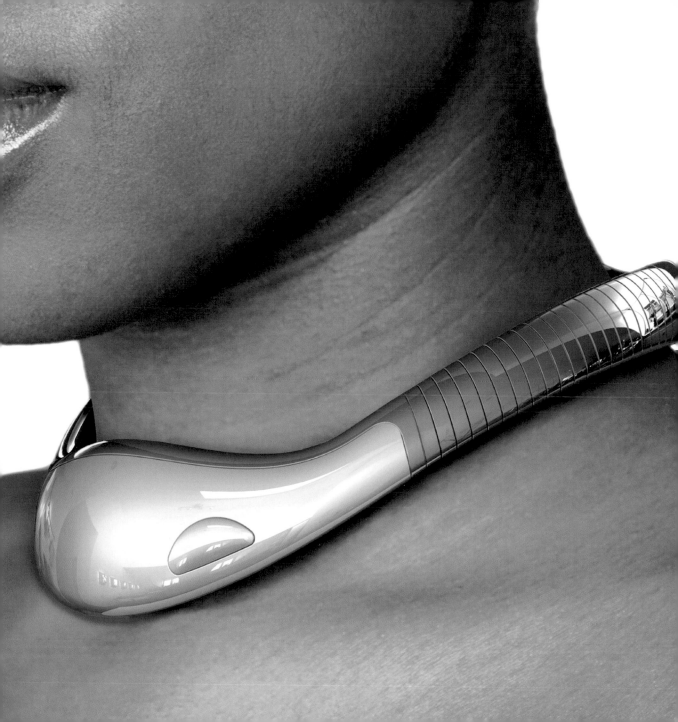

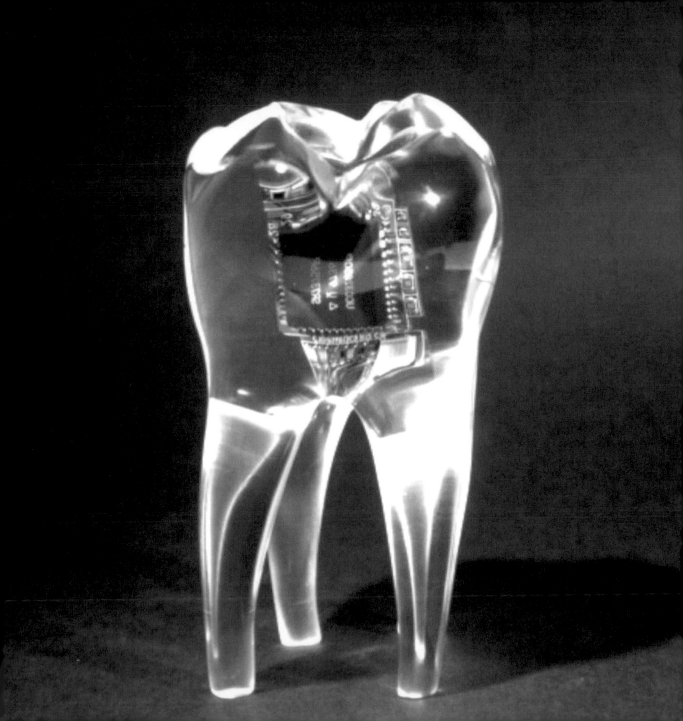

You've Got a Message Stuck in Your Teeth

You just can't live without your cell phone? Then try the molar phone. Two former students from the Royal College of Art in London, James Auger and Jimmy Loizeau, came up with the idea for a cell phone so discreet that it takes up no more space than a tooth filling. Equipped with a vibration device and a low-frequency receiver, it transmits sound to the ear through the jawbone — which allows you to make calls in complete privacy. In fact, with its placement at the back of the mouth, no one will hear your phone ring. Its inventors believe that this type of phone will be popular with traders on Wall Street and in London's City or even with football coaches, who would love to be able to communicate with their players without having the other team hear.

Audio Tooth Implant
PRICE: **PRODUCT STILL IN DEVELOPMENT**
Information: **http://www.auger-loizeau.com**

Silent Phoning

"**Q**uiet, I'm on the phone." NTT DoCoMo Inc. is working on a prototype of a telephone that can read lips. The secret of this new device is a group of three electrodes attached to the thumb and first two fingers. When touching specific points around the outside of the mouth, they can detect microelectrical activity produced by the mouth and facial muscles while speaking — or simply while mouthing words without making any actual sounds. Potential uses for the device go beyond medical applications to aid deaf mutes, or people who have temporarily lost their voices, to communicate by phone. Since background noise doesn't affect the message being sent you can make yourself understood even in a sawmill or at a heavy-metal concert. And while riding in buses or subways you can talk to friends without having to share stories about your love life — or your child's case of diarrhea — with everyone around you.

NTT DoCoMo Phone
PRICE: **PRODUCT STILL IN DEVELOPMENT**
Information: **www.newscientist.com**

Talking with Your Hands

Whether it's for regular conversations, text messaging or even video calls, designer Sunman Kwon is taking the future of communications back to its origins: the hand. That old appendage will still be useful for waving hello, giving the OK or getting the attention of servers at restaurants, but thanks to this new device it can also be transformed into a cell phone compatible with the latest data transmission standards. Still in the development stage, this communication system straps on a bit like a wristwatch and will project an interactive keyboard onto your four fingers, which, thanks to laser technology, can be used just like the 12 buttons on a normal telephone. Your thumb is left free, and you can dial or type with the fingers of your other hand — but you shouldn't try this while driving.

Finger Touching
PRICE: **PRODUCT STILL UNDER DEVELOPMENT**
Information: **http://www.yankodesign.com**

I Think, Therefore I... Can!

Using the ancestral powers of the mind, I can... move a virtual car or operate my computer. With the help of MindSet that is. Currently under development by the Silicon Valley start-up NeuroSky, these headsets have bio-captors that record brain and muscle activity and transmit the information wirelessly to a computer. The signals that are produced can be used to play traditional video games or to control characters in virtual worlds. The user's emotional state can also be detected, adding a further variable that can modify the information received by the computer. Several companies are already working on projects with MindSet, for use in video games and digital music applications. "Turn on, computer! My wish is your command!"

MindSet
PRICE: **PRODUCT STILL IN DEVELOPMENT**
Information: **http://www.neurosky.biz**

Cooling Off the Brain

Is your brain overheated? Then have it air-conditioned. A team of scientists at Yamaguchi Univerisity in Japan has filed a patent for a brain-cooling device. Sound crazy? No, in fact, it's a medical treatment. In severe cases of epilepsy, the brain can be subjected to overheating due to a high level of electrical activity in overexcited cells. The increased temperature causes even more cells to fire, thus exacerbating the situation. Implanted into the affected region, this device can help keep seizures from becoming too extreme. It consists of a special pipe connected to a heat sink outside the head, which helps cool the brain. It's a bit frightening, but it's serious stuff.

Did you know?

About 50 million people in the world suffer from epilepsy, and more than half don't have access to any form of treatment.

Brain Radiator
PRICE: **PRODUCT STILL IN DEVELOPMENT**
Information: **http://www.newscientist.com**

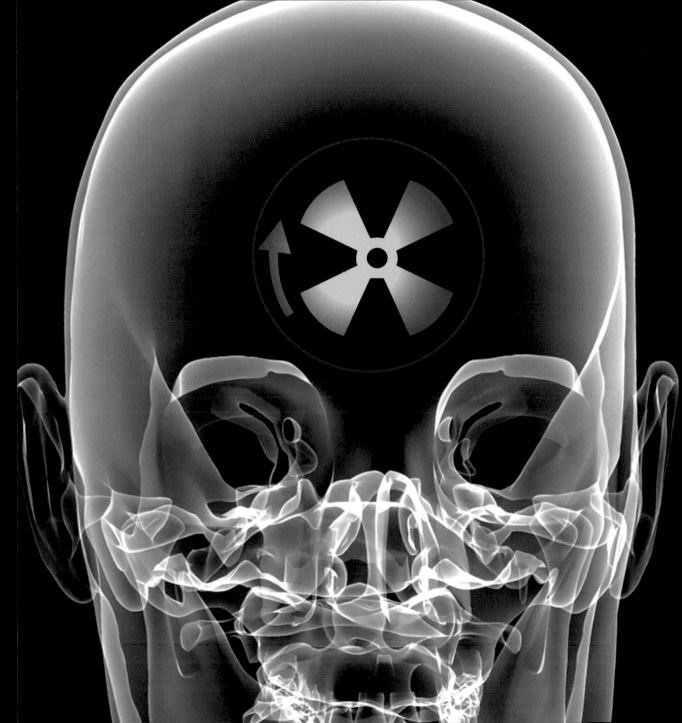

Right from the Head

A voice that comes from deep inside — words that swell up directly from thoughts. That's the dream of Erik Ramsey. Since suffering a brain stem stroke caused by a car accident, he's been a victim of what's known as locked-in syndrome. He can't move or speak, but he's conscious and totally aware of what's going on around him. Only able to communicate with eye movements, Erik Ramsey is trapped inside his own body. But in 2004 a team at Boston University implanted an electrode in his brain. For several years it's recorded a sort of diagram corresponding to sounds imagined by Erik. Soon, a program should be developed that will directly translate his silent thoughts into words that have already been waiting too long to get out.

The Mind Reader
PRICE: **PRODUCT STILL IN DEVELOPMENT**
Information: **http://speechlab.bu.edu**

Tradition Meets High-Tech

At a time when China is making rapid advances in technology, the designer Yun Liang has brought together history and high-tech in the Scroll Phone. The shape of this new communication device is directly inspired by ancient Chinese paintings done on parchment, which were kept rolled up when not being admired. The basic keyboard of this telephone, as well as the speaker, is located on the outside of a tube, allowing for simple calling. But for more complex operations you have to unroll the flexible screen.

Scroll Phone
PRICE: **UNKNOWN AT THIS TIME**
Information: **http://www.yankodesign.com**

The Rubber Cell Phone

This is twisted! The Nokia 888, dreamed up by designer Tamer Nakisci, is the most flexible phone ever. You can put it through an entire gymnastics routine or into every position in the *Kama Sutra* and it won't complain. To achieve this athletic suppleness its inventor incorporated liquid batteries, voice recognition and a flexible touch screen into its design. This telephone, which, according to Nakisci, should behave a bit like an electronic pet, can be programmed to take a particular shape whenever you want. What's more, other 888 users can send your phone forms, turning it into a heart or even making it do a small dance right before your eyes.

Nokia 888
PRICE: **PRODUCT STILL IN DEVELOPMENT**
Information: **http://www.nokia888.com**

Brave
New Inventions

The ingenuity of designers can make lamps levitate and allow you to redecorate your walls effortlessly. Technology has brought flexibility to whole a host of products, with everything from watches to partitions that can adapt to all sorts of different situations. It's inside pillows that can wake you up gently with soft light, and it's helping give you privacy at work. There's no dearth of interactivity either, as new devices aid us in choosing our clothing or remind us of appointments in a suave voice. Once the imagination of inventors starts focusing on our daily lives, there's no telling where it will go.

White Light Rising

The bright idea of Angela Jansen and the Crealev Company, this lamp will really lighten up any atmosphere. Its shade levitates peacefully above the base, serenely floating in thin air. The company, which has filed several patents, isn't revealing many details about how it is done. What they are saying is that they've developed technology that can raise objects weighing up to a pound (0.5 kg) about 2 inches (5 cm) high, using only an 8-volt power source.

Crealev
http://www.crealev.com

Advice that Reflects Well on You

This mirror shows no pity, but it really has your best interests at heart. Really. It reads RFID (radio frequency identification) tags attached to products and then displays information concerning your clothing choices on an interactive touch screen. Using information from the tag, the mirror can suggest appropriate accessories, such as the right pair of shoes to go with your dress. And if the size isn't right, with the mere touch of a finger you can send a message to the salesperson. If you still can't decide the mirror can send a picture of you in whatever you're trying on to a website where friends and family can offer their more or less helpful advice and comments.

RFID Mirror
http://www.thebigspace.com

Stuck on You

Time passes, time flies, time goes by, and you can't stop time. But you can get it to stick in one place — on you. The TimeFlex, invented by the company Solovyovdesign, is a prototype of a disposable self-adhesive liquid crystal watch. Intended for situations when wearing a regular watch is impractical or impossible, TimeFlex can be stuck on work gloves, sportswear or right on your skin. Though it doesn't look like much, the TimeFlex incorporates liquid crystals, an electronic chip and a battery all in a thin, transparent plastic strip with an adhesive backing.

TimeFlex
http://solovyovdesign.com

Mirror, Mirror, on the Wall, What Time's My Meeting at the Mall?

This mirror won't tell you if you're the fairest of them all (you know that already), but it will tell you whether Prince Charming has finally left the office and is headed back to your home sweet home. Behind this mirror's ordinary appearance is a perfect butler. It'll inform you of the arrival of any visitors, remind you of appointments and tell you when the Jacuzzi is the right temperature. With its ever so British accent and its 133 prerecorded phrases, pretty soon you'll wonder how you ever survived without it.

Magic Mirror
http://www.themeaddicts.com/pages/mirror.html

The New Score

Sheet music wasn't the most practical invention in the world. It can be bulky, and you have to turn the pages by hand — or enlist the services of someone with good ears to do it for you if you want to play without those occasional breaks in the flow. That's all over with the E-paper Music Score designed by Serina Sung. This electronic sheet music is actually a single flexible screen equipped with a Bluetooth connection that allows it to download music from a computer. Even better, you turn the virtual pages with a foot pedal. "Look Mom, no hands!".

EMS (E-Paper Music Score)
http://www.yankodesign.com

The Wake-Up Pillow

The Glo Pillow has a soul as paradoxical as the dream world itself. Its cushiony comfort helps you drift off to sleep, but its (soft) light wakes you up. It comes equipped with an alarm and an LED grid that simulates a natural sunrise (gradually increasing from 0 to 250 lux in 40 minutes) to make getting out of bed a painless process. This idea has already been used in wake-up lamps, but here it's your friendly pillow that becomes your gentle morning wake-up service.

Glo pillow
http://www.embryo.ie/glo

Laser Graffiti

"Yes dear, of course you can scribble all over the walls. Enjoy yourself!" And why not? As long as it's with Drag & Draw, a prototype laser painting system from Philips, which allows kids to go wild on the wallpaper without any risk. To get started your budding Picasso just dips his "brush" into the digital paint bucket. With each stir LEDs in the bucket light up in different colors — the child stops moving the brush when he or she has just the right hue. Then it's on to any flat surface in the house to begin a colorful masterpiece. Even better, with the wave of a magic wand an appropriate background appears and the painting becomes animated.

Drag & Draw
http://www.philips.com

Eclipsing Your Fellow Workers

If your employer hasn't yet realized that you deserve a deluxe private office and has got you out working in the middle of bustling secretaries and yakking salespeople, then the Eclipse Office is for you. Its retractable panels fan out over the desk and chair — and lighting, speakers and a webcam are incorporated into the structure. Safe inside your den, you'll have everything you need. And if you need to move, the whole thing rolls on casters.

The Eclipse Office
http://www.yankodesign.com

Hear Ye! See Ye!

If you'd like subtitles, please put on your Cesya glasses. They won't help you see any better, but they will send you messages during the show. Once they're adjusted correctly, just sit back and watch the movie, DVD or television program. Specially designed for the hearing impaired, these glasses provide personalized subtitles synchronized with the images. They work using a miniature antenna, which links the glasses to a remote computer that transmits the information up to a distance of about 150 feet (46 m).

Cesya
http://www.cesya.es/en

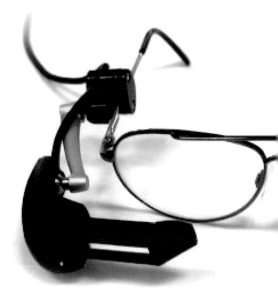

Comfy Calling

If you like talking on the phone until the wee hours of the night, then you'll love the PerCushion. The perfect accessory, it connects wirelessly to your cell phone via Bluetooth. Slightly curved, it's a real pillow with a soft foam core covered with cotton velvet. The 26-inch (66 cm) long PerCushion is equipped with a speaker and microphone so you can carry on conversations while relaxing on the sofa or even in bed. When you're finished talking you can just drift off to sleep. And even if you get lost in your dreams, you won't miss any calls since your phone will be right by your ear.

Did you know?

If you're not exactly thrilled by the idea of chatting away on the phone while lying in bed, then maybe the Sound Pillow is more your style. A bit more discreet, it limits itself to playing the music of your choice to help you fall asleep in a relaxing atmosphere ($40.00).

PerCushion
PRICE: **PRODUCT STILL IN DEVELOPMENT**
Information: **http://www.urbantool.com.au/products/percushion.asp**

The Hide-Away Bathtub

If you've got a bathroom the size of a broom closet and have given up dreaming of a hot, relaxing bubble bath — just wash your hands, remove the sink that covers the tub and run the bathwater. The answer to the prayers of apartment dwellers who can't yet afford a downtown palace, the Ladybird bath and vanity, designed by Coco Reynolds, fits a sink, countertop and bathtub into the amount of space usually taken up by a shower. Compact and sturdy, this elegant unit is made of Corian®, a nonporous material made of natural minerals and acrylic resins. With a retractable step for getting in and out of the tub with ease, it's currently available in red, black or white.

Ladybird Bath
PRICE: **AVAILABLE ON REQUEST**
Information: **http://www.cocoreynolds.com**

Freshly Washed

Start up the washer, it's stifling in here. While washing your clothes the Toshiba TW-3000VE also cools things off. Built into the back of the appliance is an air conditioner capable of bringing down the temperature of a small room. Since washing machines are often situated in areas without windows, this added feature, which keeps the air circulating, helps prevent the build-up of mold and mildew. The Toshiba-3000VE uses more water than ordinary washing machines but needs less electricity. Available in silver, gold and orange, it's sure to be welcome in Japan where in many households space is at a premium.

Toshiba TW-3000VE
PRICE: **ABOUT $2,600**
Information: **http://www.toshiba.co.jp**

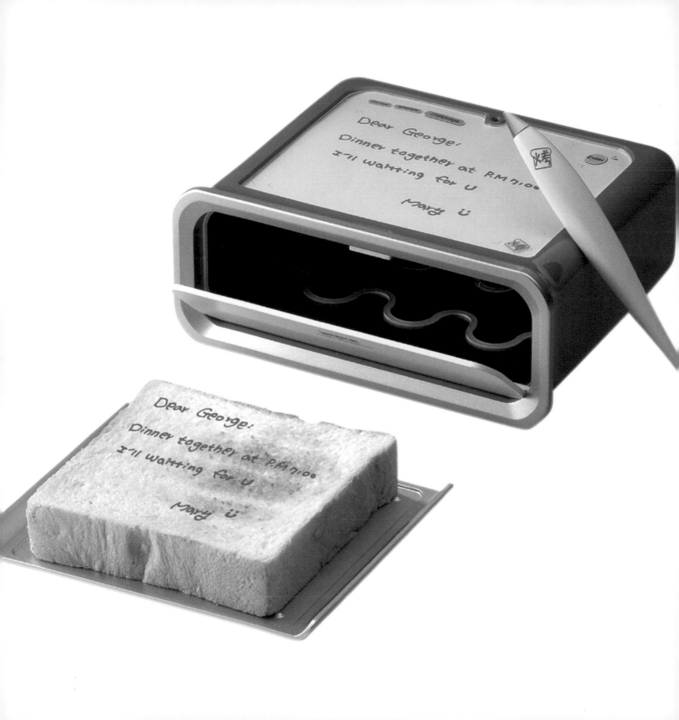

Sweet Nothings, on Toast

In the beginning was the Word, and in the beginning of the morning was breakfast. Better than a note — and a lot tastier — is the memo toaster. Invented by the designer Sasha Tseng, this appliance, which is still on the drawing board, will come equipped with an electronic notepad and a special stylus. Instead of ink it uses heat to inscribe your sweet nothings in fiery letters. With a little bit of jam on top you can convey your most important messages — "I love you," "Remember to pick up the car at the garage" or "It's over between us. Have a nice breakfast" — with incomparable sweetness.

Toast Messenger
PRICE: **PRODUCT STILL IN DEVELOPMENT**
Information: **http://fotologue.jp/Sashapure**

High-Speed Chilling Out

F ed up with the lack of space in his fridge for the really important stuff (drinks!), New Zealand student Kent Hodgson invented a small, totally portable device that can cool down any liquid in less than half a minute without diluting it. This thin tubular gadget (which fits, by the way, into the neck of a typical beer bottle), is activated when the cooling chambers are pressed down into the dock containing liquid carbon dioxide. When the CO_2 expands it forms extremely cold dry ice inside the chambers. Then all you do is pop it into your drink and wait a few seconds. According to Hodgson, a single cartridge can cool about 30 12-ounce (355 ml) beverages, at a cost of around seven cents each. So for your next picnic throw out the cooler and use the extra space for more beer.

Huski
PRICE: **ABOUT $50**
Information: **http://inventorspot.com**

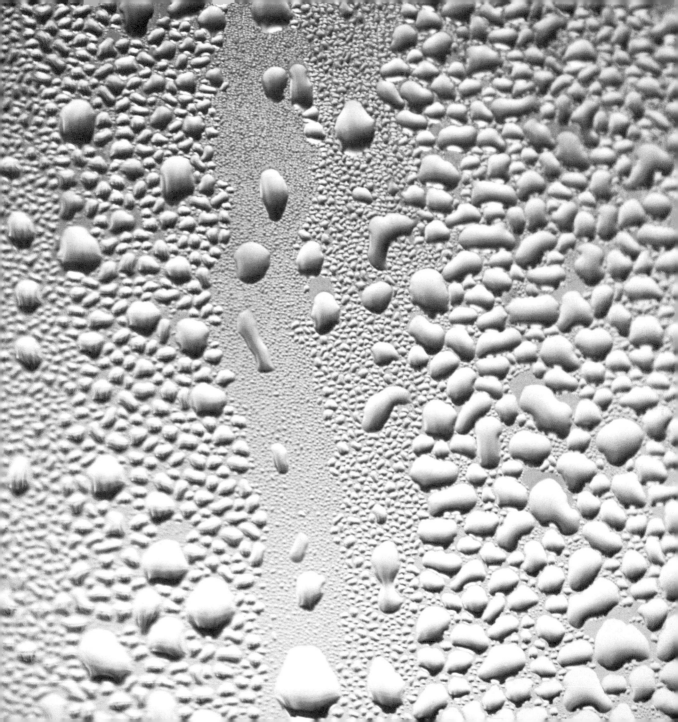

EAT
ME

One Smart Egg

Lion Quality Egg producers are in the process of developing a self-timing egg. It tells you when it's cooked. The process is actually very simple: the company's logo, printed on the shell with heat-sensitive ink, appears once the egg is done. They come in three "models": soft-boiled (ready in 3 minutes), medium-boiled (5 minutes) and hard-boiled (7 minutes). Welcome to the world of the "thermochromic" egg. Now you just have to make sure you don't mix up the three different kinds.

Did you know?

Ben Harris, an Irish student, has taken a different approach to getting his soft-boiled eggs just right. He's invented the perfEGG, which cooks up to perfection after eight and a half minutes through a process that keeps the water at a constant temperature, below the boiling point.

Lion Quality Egg
PRICE: **PRODUCT STILL IN DEVELOPMENT**
Information: **http://www.britegg.co.uk**

What did the Fridge say to the Stove?

When a fridge meets another appliance, what's their conversation like? Shop talk? More likely a kitchen klatch. In the future refrigerators will be able to speak stove fluently, and the pantry will be gossiping with the wine cellar. Their discussions, however, will remain focused on practical, household concerns and entirely devoted to your well-being and, above all, your "well-eating." Researchers have been working on helping everyday appliances communicate. Refrigerators, for example, will be able to take inventory and place an order on the Internet when you run out of eggs. General Electric has developed an entire intelligent kitchen that will inform you of what foods you have on hand, suggest meal menus that can be made with them and take care of ordering what's needed. And, like a good nanny, it can even remind you to take an umbrella if it's cloudy as well as record family members' audio and video messages. Pretty good for kitchen help.

GE Intelligent Kitchen
PRICE: **PRODUCT STILL IN DEVELOPMENT**
Information: **http://www.geappliances.com**

The Magic Box

Of course it'll all fit in there. You just have to fold it right and know how to stack. Designers Marcel Krings and Sebastian Mühlhäuse have figured out how to put an entire room's worth of furniture into a single box that is compact and light enough to be carried by two people. And it all unpacks in a matter of minutes. First step: fold back the sides to form a large rectangular structure that looks like something you might store your clothes in. Second, third, fourth and nth step: take out cube after cube of various sizes and shapes, boards of different lengths and things that unfold left and right, then assemble it all using nothing more than you hands. In less than 10 minutes (according to the company), right before you eyes will appear a bookcase, a table, a bed with mattress (a folding bed, of course), a stool, a desk with drawers, a wardrobe and two night tables that double as seats. Incredible.

Casulo
PRICE: **PRODUCT STILL IN DEVELOPMENT**
Information: **http://www.mein-casulo.de**

Light Sleeper

As you drift off to sleep you get carried away to a world of dreams where anything is possible — where beds can fly. And why should a bed have its feet on the ground, anyway? The Floating Bed seems detached from everything, especially the floor. It hovers at about 16 inches (40 cm) off the ground, as if ready to take off for the future. Maintained in this state of levitation by magnetic forces produced by elements in the floor and kept in position by thin steel cables, this bed, according to its designers, is "a metaphor for intelligent life." It was inspired by the monolith in Stanley Kubrick's *2001, A Space Odyssey*. But is it really a bed? This fascinating and eerie black rectangle could just as well serve as a table or sofa. Or it could simple play its own role of a monolith that seems to have fallen out of the sky.

Floating Bed
PRICE: **PRODUCT STILL IN DEVELOPMENT**
Information: **http://www.universearchitecture.com**

The Robot that Sticks with You

It's called the Hybrid Assistive Limb, but you can call it. HAL, a semi-cyborg. An actual robot that you wear, HAL can help you walk or even run. But it wasn't designed to transform your average guy into the $6 million dollar man who can run 60 miles (95 km) per hour or lift the front end of a car. In fact, it's designed to give energy and mobility to people with disabilities such as polio.

Did you know?

While Japan is working on solutions to cope with its aging population,
the United States is considering using this type of robot for their military,
to give soldiers greater strength and make certain tasks easier.

HAL (Hybrid Assistive Limb)
PRICE: **ESTIMATED AT $19,000, ONCE READY FOR MARKET**
Information: **http://sanlab.kz.tsukuba.ac.jp/english/r_hal.php**

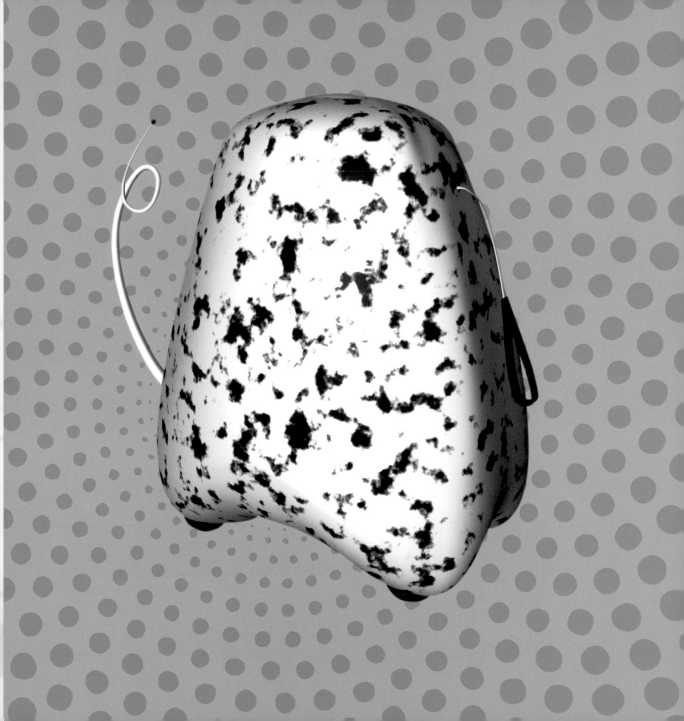

The Robot Suitcase

Have you had enough of dragging your luggage through crowded airports? Tony the robot suitcase will change all that. All you need to do is carry a special electronic card in your pocket or purse and the suitcase will follow you everywhere. Equipped with detectors to help it avoid obstacles, even in crowded situations, this new suitcase can run on uneven surfaces without problem. But Tony has competition... It's Fido, the suitcase that heels. It works on the same basic principle as Tony, but faithful Fido recognizes its master's voice, and if you somehow get separated from each other, an integrated GPS helps you find your lost luggage. For the moment the design does not include a "sic-'em" function. Both of these robotic suitcases are expected to be available in 2009, but their specification sheets don't indicate if they'll make it through customs.

Tony and Fido
PRICE: **ABOUT $2,000**
Information: **http://www.robotronic.ru** or **http://www.yeadon.net**

Ask the Table!

Intuiface is a great help with work and a real charmer at get-togethers with friends. From now on your table will have a sharp mind and a friendly personality. Its surface is a large touch screen that several people can use at the same time, which is a lot of fingers on the table. You can visualize and manipulate a great variety of information (including texts, images, video and sound) and do it as a group. So roll up your sleeves, gather round the table — and let you fingers do the working.

Intuiface
PRICE: **FROM $15,000 TO $23,750**
Information: **http://www.intuiface.com**

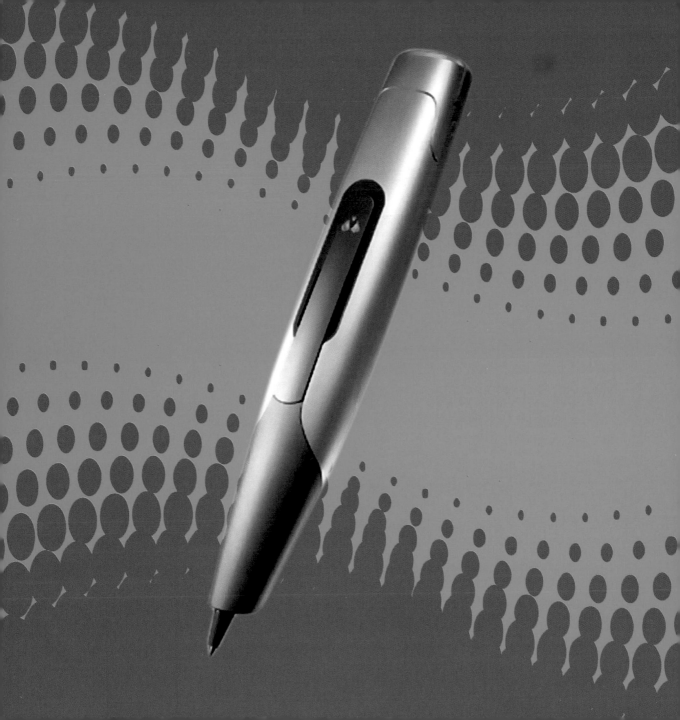

Automatic Writing

The Fly Fusion pen is inspired by the principle of "augmented reality." It allows you to write as you would with a normal pen, but thanks to its interaction with specially designed Fly Paper, it can transform your chicken scratch into beautiful typed documents. While that is it's main function, this little device can also play music from an Mp3 unit and quiz you on math or history. And with additional software it can even help you with your homework. If you write a word in English you'll hear it right away in Spanish or French.

Fly Fusion Pentop Computer
PRICE: **ABOUT $80**
Information: **http://www.flyworld.com**

The Talking Note

Flowers, chocolates or that really unique paperweight all make great gifts, but choosing cards to go with them can be a nightmare. If your eyes start to glaze over as you look at the racks and racks of syrupy sentiments, try something new: the Voca Patch. About the size of a standard sticky note, it's equipped with an electronic chip capable of recording a 12-second message. With an adhesive back it'll stick on anything — including gift wrap. The lucky recipient just has to press "play" to hear your personalized message. Look out Hallmark!

VocaPatch
PRICE: **ABOUT $7**

The Postcard of Tomorrow

With Snap+Send some day you'll be able to put a whole photo album in a postcard. This device, invented by Australian student Stuart Calvey, is actually a thin 2-megapixel digital camera incorporating a battery, screen and memory. Once you've taken 32 pictures you just put a stamp on the thing and drop it in a mailbox. The recipient just has to push a button on this high-tech post card to see a mini-slideshow, or they can transfer the images to a computer. It's much better than a picture of a palm tree you never actually saw and an only half believable, "Wish you were here."

Snap+Send
PRICE: **PRODUCT STILL IN DEVELOPMENT**
Information: **http://www.fbe.unsw.edu.au**

Pictures that Send You Spinning

No film, no batteries, no wires — but it almost looks like it's smiling and saying "cheese!" It's the Odo Twirl N' Take from Sony. This digital camera made out of recycled plastic is shaped a bit like a pizza cutter, and you have to roll it for about 15 seconds to charge it up enough to take a picture. Due to its minimalist design and its green spirit, it's a bit austere: there's no viewing screen or advanced functions. And since it has a poetic and ecologically friendly nature, when it's not being used the Twirl N' Take fits into a holder shaped like a flowerpot.

Did you know?

The Twirl N' Take is just one member of the Odo family of products.
There's also the Crank N' Capture, a camera you wind up, the Juice Box, a solar battery,
and the Pull N' Play, stereo headphones with a built-in radio that are powered by pulling a cord.

Odo Twirl N' Take
PRICE: **PRODUCT STILL IN DEVELOPMENT**
Information: **http://www.sony.net/fun/design**

Renewed
Energy

Nature inspires science. The warmth of the sun, the blowing wind — everything is becoming a potential source of energy. New products are creating a world where batteries run on water or bacteria or charge up using the power of sugar, like plants. It's a whole new universe, where the sun slowly cooks your chicken dinner and the wind keeps your cell phone from going dead. Humans themselves can be the source of their own energy — with body heat or muscle movement generating electricity for all sorts of devices. That way you'll never be caught without power.

Power Source with a Place in the Sun

There's nothing new under the sun — or is there? To protect yourself from harmful UV rays that come streaming through the holes in the ozone while at the same time combating global warming, try the Sun-brella. Invented by Greg Freer, it combines the features of a beach umbrella and solar panels. The photovoltaic cells let you run small electric appliances, up to 282 watts, but you can also cool yourself off with the Sun-brella's built-in fan.

Sun-brella
http://www.yankodesign.com

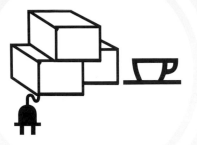

Pass Me Your Soda, My Battery's Dead!

Sony has come up with a sugar-powered battery. The casing, made of vegetable-based plastic, is in the form of a white cube about an inch and half (4 cm) on each side. Filled with a sugar solution, the battery generates power using the same principle as living organisms: a bacteria burns glucose, thus creating electricity. Enzymes are used as a catalyst to start the process. Sony claims that the product was inspired by photosynthesis.

Bio Battery
http://www.sony.net

Single Battery Seeking Cute Liquid for an Energizing Relationship

It's finally here: the ecological battery. It contains no pollutants, and it charges up with any liquid. You just have to fill it using the pipette that comes with it. The liquid, preferably water, is transformed into energy with help of a catalyst contained in the battery. They can deliver 1.5 volts for about 20 hours and are priced at $6 each. The strange sounding name of this battery is NoPoPo, which stands for No Pollution Power. The manufacturer claims that, in an emergency, it'll even work with saliva or urine.

NoPoPo
http://www.aps-j.jp/english/index.htm

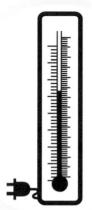

The Body Electric

The Fraunhofer Research Institute has developed "thermoelectric" generators. They can transform the temperature difference between the human body and the surrounding environment into energy. These special generators use what would otherwise be wasted heat to create electricity.

Body heat electricity
http://www.fraunhofer.de

Dancing as if the World Depended on It

Go out to a nightclub? Help protect the environment? The Sustainable Dance Club allows you to do both. The floor absorbs the movements of the dancers and transforms them into electricity used for lighting. The club also captures rainwater for the restrooms, has windmills and solar panels on the roof and uses low-wattage LED illumination. So protect the environment and dance! The club is also working on a system to capture dancers' sweat and recycle it for use in flushing the toilets.

Sustainable Dance Club
http://www.sustainabledanceclub.com

More Light than You Can Shake a Stick At

Light up your life — it's all in the wrist action. "Eternal" ecological flashlights work using a strong magnet. You just shake them, and the magnet moves back and forth through a coil, charging up a condenser with electricity. There's no limit to the number of times they can be recharged. So get shakin'.

Shake-powered flashlight
http://www.gadgetshop.com

The Power T-Shirt

Researchers at the Georgia Institute of Technology in Atlanta have developed a new fabric that uses the movements of the person wearing it to produce electricity. This project, still in the experimental stage, aims at creating clothes that double as mini power plants. Kevlar fibers are covered with zinc oxide nanowires. When the fibers rub together they cause a current to flow through a metal coating. For the moment the amount of electricity produced is very small, but further research should lead to improvements.

Electricity-generating thread
http://technology.newscientist.com

Here Comes the Sun

The Solar Cooker designed by Koo Ho Shin is an appliance that has a special relationship with the sun. Food is placed under a glass globe in the middle. To get the meal started, unfold the reflective petals surrounding the globe. The sun takes cares of the cooking. To adjust the temperature all you have to do is change the angle of the petals, which allows you to reposition the focal point and make sure that everything comes out just the way you like it.

Solar cooker
http://pasly.com

Calling on the Wind

As long as there's a good wind you won't have to worry about your cell phone battery going dead. Orange in Great Britain has launched the first wind-powered phone charger. This independent mini-turbine generates electricity that is then stored in a control box. You just connect you phone to it whenever it needs charging.

Orange cell phone wind charger
http://www.orange.co.uk

The Ecological Detective

Everything seems to be going green, and this little box that keeps track of you energy consumption will make sure it stays that way. Not content with monitoring every little activity in the house, it also lets you and everyone else know how you're doing — in bright colored lights. The LED screen turns blue if you're behaving like the perfect tree hugger, but if you start getting wasteful it sees (and shows) red. And there's no excuse for not getting one of these useful devices since it's simple to install. Its receptor-emitter connects between the electric meter and your home's circuit breakers. The screen is wireless, so you can move it around and keep an eye on your ecological report card anywhere in the house.

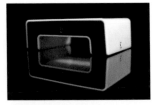

Did you know?

Wattson's inseparable companion, Holmes, is a computer program that saves your energy consumption data and allows you to compare your results to those of other users via the Internet.

Wattson
PRICE: $260
Information: http://www.diykyoto.com

A Motorbike that Really Swings

This'll catch your eye if you see it go by. The City Swing is a sleek apple green motorbike with dual front wheels and room for three. Gert-Jan Van Breugel, the industrial designer behind the project, sees it as the taxi of the future. Smaller than normal taxis, the City Swing will be able to speed through heavy city traffic, making use of bus lanes and spaces too small for other vehicles. Yet it's large enough to take two passengers and all their stuff. And this motorbike isn't just green on the outside — nicknamed "The Green Taxi," it's designed to run on biofuel or electricity. Soon you'll be swinging through traffic jams.

City Swing
PRICE: **PRODUCT STILL IN DEVELOPMENT**
Information: **http://www.gjvanbreugel.nl**

A Green Boat for the Blue Ocean

It sails along like a sleek fish — and seen from afar it looks as though it could take off and fly. This futuristic and environmentally friendly boat is called the Volitan, and it's the brainchild of the Turkish company Design Nobis. The vessel's solar panels and an integrated computer give it a high-tech edge on traditional sailboats. As long as there's wind the boat can move along under the power of its rigid sails, and during the day the solar panels, which cover both sides of the sails, produce electricity that can be stored in the boat's batteries. If the wind dies down the Volitan can keep on sailing thanks to dual propellers driven by electric motors that are powered by the batteries. Designed with safety in mind, the boat can operate in winds of up to 60 knots, and two "floating wings" give added stability to the craft.

Did you know?

The Volitan is named for a real flying fish of the tropics, the *Exocoetus volitans*. Its fins allow it to jump out of the water and glide through the air for short distances, an ability that helps it escape from predators.

Volitan
PRICE: **PRODUCT STILL IN DEVELOPMENT**
Information: **http://www.designnobis.com**

The High-Rise Farm

Get in the elevator — we're going to the farm! With the Vertical Farm project skyscraper meets landscaper. In other words, it's a high-rise building transformed into a fully functioning farm. The first to 10th floors are the home to cackling chickens and mooing cows; the next 20 floors provide growing space for grains, fruits and vegetables. Starting from the realization that, by 2050, 80 percent of the earth's population will live in cities, the Vertical Farm project at Columbia University aims to attain food supply self-sufficiency for urban centers. The researchers at Columbia estimate that 150 farms of this type would be enough to take care of the food needs of a city such as New York.

Did you know?

This concept is designed to be environmentally friendly. By minimizing the space used to raise livestock or grow crops it helps preserve forestlands. What's more, the vertical farms use renewable energy sources.

Vertical Farm
PRICE: **PRODUCT STILL IN DEVELOPMENT**
Information:: **www.verticalfarm.com**

Vegetables Fresh from the Kitchen Sink

Why go to the supermarket when you can transform your kitchen into a well-watered garden? The Miele Cultivate System uses hydroponics to help you grow fruits and vegetables at home. Rather than soil, the plants grow in an inert medium, such as clay pebbles, and are irrigated with recycled water enriched with mineral nutrients. It's decorative, full of vitamins and it's good for the planet. The project's designer, Eoin McNally, sees this type of mini-garden as an aesthetic way to reduce the tons of fuel used every day to transport fruits and vegetables from distant farms to the supermarket and then home. Hydroponics also uses much less water than traditional farming. So get planting. Your kitchen will be more beautiful, your meals more delicious and the earth a little greener.

Miele Cultivate System
PRICE: **PRODUCT STILL IN DEVELOPMENT**
Information: **http://www.embryo.ie/miele/index.html**

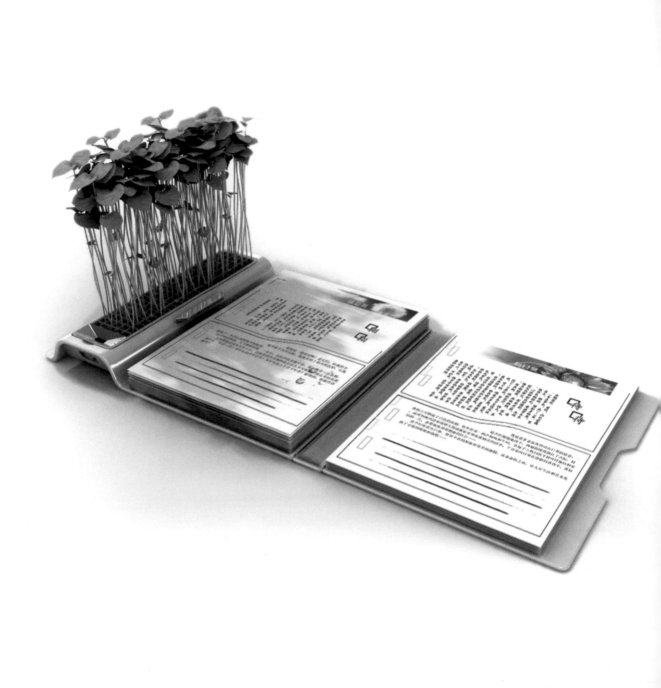

Helping Your Mind Grow

As you turn the pages you cultivate your garden So that reading would germinate more than just ideas, designer Eric Zhang invented the Book on Life. Attached to the left-hand side of the cover is a place where readers can plant whatever kinds of seeds they want — whatever inspires them — and then watch them grow as they pursue their intellectual journey. To add an extra touch of magic to this new kind of book, small LEDs placed near the bottom of the plants transform it into a unique lamp, whose soft light reflects off the green leaves. Zhang's goal is that readers "not only learn the meaning of life," but "create life themselves." Not bad for a book.

Book of Life
PRICE: **PRODUCT STILL IN DEVELOPMENT**
Information: **http://www.yankodesign.com**

Flowering Conversations

All those innocent-looking cell phones are actually born polluters: each one includes a plastic case made out of petrochemicals and electronics loaded with heavy metals such as nickel, lithium and mercury. The University of Warwick in Great Britain, in conjunction with Motorola, has developed a cell phone with a green heart. Made of biodegradable polymers, it will slowly disintegrate in any compost pile. Even better, it blooms — embedded in the case, behind a little plastic window is a dwarf sunflower seed just waiting to be dropped in the soil and start growing. Of course the electronic components and the screen still aren't biodegradable, but this is a telephone that speaks to our ecological conscience. And it says it with flowers.

Did you know?

In Great Britain 1,700 cell phones are thrown away every hour. In Australia over 10 million phones have been discarded. And worldwide, just the electronics in old cell phones add up to 50 million tons a year.

Biodegradable Phone
PRICE: **PRODUCT STILL IN DEVELOPMENT**
Information: **http://www2.warwick.ac.uk/**

Moon Dew

When it's that time of the month some women refer to their moonflow or moonblood. It lasts for about 3 to 7 days, but normally it's referred to more prosaically as their period. The problem is that the tampons and sanitary napkins that get used during this period are helping destroy the world's forests. Soon, however, women will be able to make a choice more in harmony with nature by using the Moon Cup. This charming little menstrual cup is made of hypoallergenic silicone and measures about 2 inches (5 cm) long. It safely collects menstrual fluids, "without leaks or odors," according the manufacturer. You do, however, have to empty it out and rinse it every four to eight hours. But the survival of the planet is worth a little extra dishwashing, isn't it?

Moon Cup
PRICE: **ABOUT $40**
Information: **http://www.mooncup.com**

Water, Water, Everywhere

Have a glass of water, Max Water that is: cool, fresh water that comes right out of thin air. The Australian researcher Max Whisson has developed a system to produce water from ambient air using a turbine containing refrigerants. The temperature difference produces condensation, and the water droplets that form are collected in a recipient. The whole compact device runs on wind power. The Max Water just may be the solution to worldwide water shortages that already affect 400 million people and will affect close to 4 billion by 2050.

Did you know?

While he was working on this project, Dr. Whisson was inspired by the Stenocara, a little beetle that lives in the Namib Desert. In order to survive in that extremely dry environment it makes use of its forward wings. Covered with tiny sloping bumps, they capture humidity from the air and transform it into water droplets.

Max Water
PRICE: **PRODUCT STILL IN DEVELOPMENT**
Information: **http://www.waterunlimited.com.au**

Fresh from the Sewer

Stagnant water, contaminated water, wastewater. The most essential element for human survival can sometimes turn into an enemy, carrying pollutants or diseases like cholera. And that's exactly the problem Michael Pritchard wants to solve. He's invented a filtration bottle for campers, travelers, soldiers, disaster victims or anyone who doesn't have access to a safe water supply. It transforms any water poured into it into sterile drinking water. The Lifesaver Bottle 4000 can filter 4,000 liters (1,055 gallons) of water using an ultra-fine filtering system that eliminates all contaminants measuring over 15 nanometers. That means it will remove not only bacteria, but also viruses, fungi, parasites and other waterborne pathogens — in fact anything that can turn the source of life into a deadly liquid.

Lifesaver Bottle
PRICE: **ABOUT $375**
Information: **http://www.lifesaversystems.com**

Something in the Air

It smells deliciously like... nothing. "Entrée d'air" is odorless, colorless and tasteless — but it transports you to another world. In fact, this designer bottle is the home version of the oxygen bar. It contains pressurized air taken from exotic sites like the rain forests of South America or the top of Mont Fuji in Japan. And it's good for you. Breathing these pure and natural airs will clear your mind, relieve migraines and reduce stress. To add just the right touch to the atmosphere, when the bottled is tapped an inner rod begins to glow, slowly fading as the air is consumed. For about 10 to 15 minutes, with a plastic tube elegantly placed in your nose, you — or you and that someone special — can breathe a moment of serenity.

Did you know?

For its designer, Theo Aldridge, Entrée d'air offers a healthy alternative to cigars or cigarettes at the end of a dinner with friends. There's nothing like it to help you relax and feel refreshed after a meal without sacrificing your health.

Entrée d'air
PRICE: **PRODUCT STILL IN DEVELOPMENT**
Information: **http://www.yankodesign.com**

The Sheep-Mower

Get ready for a real technological leap mounted on four hoofed feet. This revolutionary lawnmower doesn't need electricity, gasoline or batteries — not even solar panels. Even better: it runs by itself without the slightest effort on your part. Just stretch out under the shade of your favorite tree and watch it go to work, cutting away all the weeds and wild grass that have been taking over your lawn and garden. Made up of a team of four valiant — and hungry — sheep in the prime of life, this mower will have your lawn done in no time. And the cut grass goes directly into the animals' stomachs, so there's no need for raking. Scientific studies have shown that this 4-headed, 16-footed lawnmower (the basic model) will even give milk. What'll they think of next?

The Mowing Machine
PRICE AND INFORMATION: **SEE YOUR NEAREST SHEPHERD**

crazy
world

Is there any limit to madness? If you've got this far in the book you're probably starting to wonder. In the space of just a few pages you've seen a jellyfish house, met a dog that lives like a prince in a palace, wandered the seabed with your head in a bubble and slept in a hotel that takes you back to the austere, red days of the Cold War. You can't hold back the progress of dementedness — in fact, things just keep getting stranger all the time. Sometimes it gets to be in pretty bad taste, violating some of society's most sacred taboos — and sometimes it's all about grandiose projects whose goal seems to be simply making things bigger and bigger, without ever questioning whether it makes any sense. If each person has an idea of what's crazy and what isn't, it's a fairly safe bet that things like supersonic toilets, ironing in a hot-air balloon or on a cow and an inflatable church that allows evangelism to take to the road in a whole new way are all pretty well placed in the running as far as eccentric ideas go. The world is crazy, and it seems to be going out of its way to prove it. There are even people trying to sell us nothing. Real, authentic nothing — guaranteed 100 percent empty. Stop and take a deep breath. Even madness knows how to relax once in a while.

Instant Love

Bragging Brian and Macho Mike will no longer be able to claim they can't find condoms big enough for guys as well endowed as they are. A German company is developing a revolutionary spray-on prophylactic. The can-type device applies liquid latex from all sides to form a protective coating that solidifies in about five seconds. Available in several colors, this customized condom fits like a glove and won't slip — or slop. Expected to be available in 2009.

Spray-on Condom
PRICE: BETWEEN $22 AND $36
Information: http://medgadget.com

Spray-On-Condom

The Down Under Ego Booster

The Ball Lifter represents a big step toward greater sexual equality — and the eradication of inferiority complexes. The masculine equivalent of the Wonderbra, it allows the wearer to discreetly highlight what he's got. This sexy accessory comes in a variety of colors to go with whatever you're wearing underneath, and there are several different models, including "adjustable" and "sport" versions and the "Ball Lifter Slip Pouch." You'll have no reason to be shy about going to the pool or the beach any more.

Did you know?

Like the Wonderbra, the Ball Lifter shouldn't be worn every day.
Too frequent usage can lead to tissue damage and lower sperm counts.

Ball Lifter
PRICE: **$17 FOR THE BASIC MODEL ; $20 FOR THE ADJUSTABLE VERSION**
Information : **http://wildmant.com**

"Chew me!"

Alice in Wonderland meets the world of Viagra when she finds a box of Bust-Up lying on the table. This incredible product contains a magic formula: pueraria mirifica. A plant from Thailand, which is supposed to have extraordinary effects on the feminine figure, it's the secret ingredient in the rosy chewing gum hidden in the box. "Chew me!" the whole bunch of them seem to shout. "Chew me, and chew me some more!" Alice loses herself in fanciful visions of increasing her breast size by 80 percent and of firmer, more beautiful knockers. She stares dreamily at the box... but she doesn't end up taking any because while these things might help your profile, they're a real risk to your health.

Did you know?

Pueraria mirifica isn't a literary invention; it's a genuine tuber found in Southeast Asia. It contains phytoestrogens, natural compounds similar to certain female hormones. If Bust-Up Gum really contains these chemical extracts — and not just snake oil — you still need to be careful. Chewing too many will multiply the number of cells in the breast — and your chances of getting cancer.

Bust-Up
PRICE: **$44 FOR 60 PIECES OF GUM (NOT DOCTOR RECOMMENDED)**
Information: **http://www.getbustupgum.com**

The Super-Clean Pick-Me-Up

One hot coffee under the shower comin' up! Shower Shock is the first caffeinated soap. Releasing an average of $^1/_{125}$ ounce (200 mg) of caffeine per use, this new product is the hygienic equivalent of two cups of coffee. How does it work? Easy, since caffeine can be absorbed through the skin. A little rub-a-dub-dub (without milk or sugar), and you're ready to go. According to the manufacturer, the energizing effect kicks in just a few minutes after use and lasts about four hours. One bar of soap is good for about 12 power showers. What's more, it really cleans the skin. And you won't end up smelling like old coffee grinds — Shower Shock is scented with peppermint oil.

Did you know?

Due to the possible effects of caffeine absorbed through the skin, this soap is not recommended for children or pregnant women.

Shower Shock
PRICE: **ABOUT $7**
Information: **http://www.thinkgeek.com**

Holding It In

In the wonderful world of princesses and knights in shining armor there's no drooling or wiping your nose — and there's definitely no farting. But in the real world of ordinary human beings, flatulence is a fact of life, often exacerbated by certain illnesses. The solution to avoid the anxiety associated with having gas — and to avoid stinking up the air — has finally arrived: Under-Ease underwear. Made of polyurethane-coated nylon, they're not exactly elegant, but they do work. This special material, with sewn-in elastic, prevents any odor from escaping. Gas is expelled through an "exit hole" and into a pocket with a replaceable filter containing activated charcoal. Nothing is lost, but everything's deodorized. There are men's, women's and unisex versions.

Did you know?

In 2001 Buck Weimer, the inventor of this anti-flatulence underwear, was the recipient of an Ig Nobel Prize, which is awarded each year for weird inventions or discoveries.

Under-Ease
PRICE: **ABOUT $30**
Information: **www.under-tec.com**

Taking Care
of Business

Ah, Japan! Noh theater, geishas, manga comic books and best of all... the toilets! Without a doubt they're the most memorable part of every tourist's visit. The land of the rising sun has become the specialist in high-tech toilets, making the West and its perfumed triple-ply paper ancient history. Because here, the toilets can do everything — or almost: there are miniature water jets that wash your private parts and seats that are not only heated to protect your rear end from a cold shock, but they lift up automatically thanks to special detectors. And for those who like to be discreet, some are equipped with speakers to help mask any bodily noises from those outside.

Sim Jae Duck was born in a bathroom. His mother thought that that would ensure him a long and prosperous life. It looks like she was right, since he's now 74 years old and president of the World Toilet Association. Duck's enthusiasm for porcelain fixtures reached new heights when he built his home... in the shape of a toilet. The house is available for rent at $50,000 a night. The money will be used to provide better toilet facilities and improve sanitation throughout the world.
Haewoojae
http://en.wtaa.or.kr

The Traveler's Toilet

What can you do to avoid public toilets, those dicey, smelly, sometimes frightening places? By taking your own personal padded toilet along with you. The Gotta Go Briefcase — perfect for the executive with no time to fart around — is elegantly appointed with mahogany leather, toilet paper dispenser and a newspaper holder. There is, however, the slight problem of odor. The inventor recommends the use of air freshener. Probably not a bad idea.

Gotta Go Briefcase
http://inventorspot.com/gotta_go

The Real Men's Room

Urinating in the men's room at the Sofitel Hotel in Queenstown, New Zealand, drives the women wild. Don't look for a feeling of privacy here — life-size photos of six young beauties checking out your equipment confront any guy who needs to go. And these women, who stare at, photograph or even measure your anatomy are likely to leave a lasting impression. So when are they going to redecorate the ladies' room?

Queenstown Sofitel Men's Room
http://www.sofitelqueenstown.com

The Toilet that Never Gets Jammed Up

Stuck in a traffic jam and really need to go? Just unpack your portable toilet. All you need to do is unfold the cardboard bowl, spread out the absorbant lining and draw the curtain that comes with it. Then you can take care of your business.

Kurumarukun
http://www.kaneko.co.jp/eindex.htm

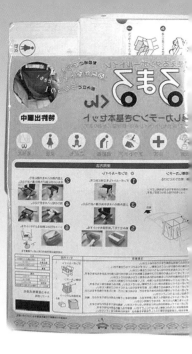

High-Tech Toilets

The makers of Japanese toilets are transforming these classic porcelain fixtures into veritable laboratories that perform all sorts of medial tests. Using a simple urine sample — which they don't have any trouble obtaining — intelligent toilets can measure your blood pressure, body mass and sugar level. They can even take your pulse. Soon they'll be able to send the results directly to your doctor through a wireless Internet connection.

Le Trone
http://www.letrone.com/index

When You Gotta Eat, You Gotta Eat

Y ou've no doubt been looking for a bathroom large enough to eat in. Search no more. The Taipei restaurant chain Toilet Bowl has realized your dream. They've created the first toilet-themed restaurant. It's a bit surprising, but customers love it. Instead of chairs you sit on toilets — a bit jazzed up, however, with multicolored seat covers. Dishes are served in miniature toilet bowls, and the glass-topped tables are supported by bathtubs and sinks. Wall decorations and lighting incorporate showers and urinals, and on the menu you'll find cute little allusions to the little boys' and little girls' rooms. There are already a dozen of these restaurants in Taiwan, some of which can "seat" up to a hundred customers, each with his or her own porcelain throne.

Toilet Bowl
Information: **http://www.coolhunting.com**

The Supersonic Toilet

The mechanic Paul Stender has come up with an invention that makes using a "Johnny-on-the-Spot" a bit more interesting. By adding a Boeing jet engine to the back and wheels underneath, he's created the fastest portable toilet in the world. From the outside it looks like any other outhouse, but when you flush, huge fireballs shoot out of this contraption that sends you barreling along at about 70 miles (113 km) per hour.

Jet Outhouse
PRICE: **ABOUT $10,000 TO BUILD**
Information: **http://www.speedforhire.com**

Humming Down the Highway

Turn right at the traffic light and then left after 800 feet of music. In Japan, Shizuo Shinoda has come up with a "melody road" that plays music when you drive over it The concept is as simple as a music box or a barrel organ: a certain number of grooves are cut into the road surface, and when a car passes over them it creates vibrations and resonance. By varying the distance between the grooves, different tones can be produced — and you can play a little tune in about 30 seconds. There have already been several melody roads set up in Japan, indicated by street signs and colorful musical notes painted on the asphalt. For optimal sound you should drive at 28 miles (45 km) per hour, otherwise the tempo will be a bit too lento or a bit too allegro. Now they just need to redo the landscape to go with the music — and make sure they don't choose corny hits.

Melody Road in Japan
AVAILABILITY: THERE ARE MELODY ROADS IN THE
PROVINCES OF HOKKAIDO, WAKAYAMA AND GUNMA

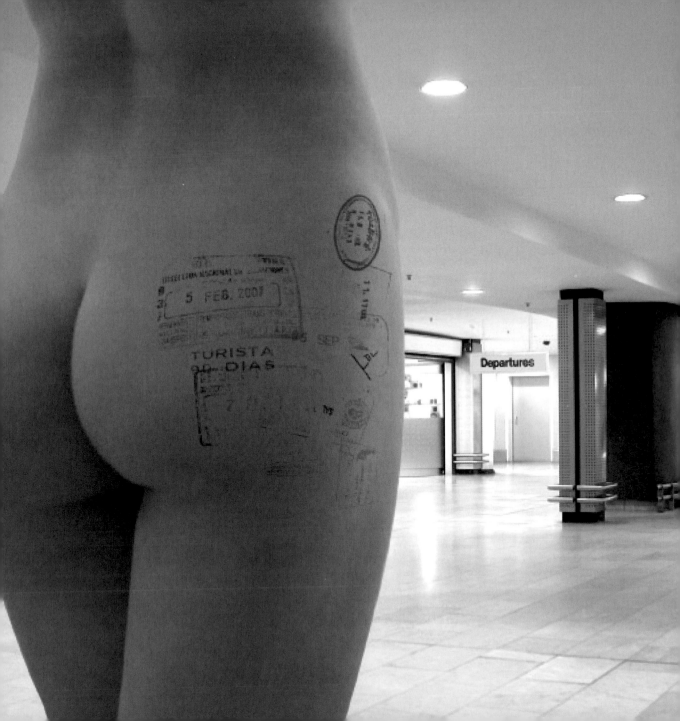

Totally Naked and Ready for Takeoff

Travelling light? In May 2003 Castaways Travel offered a nudist vacation package including a roundtrip flight from Miami to Cancun, Mexico. This breath of fresh air for the whole epidermis began in the airplane itself and was followed by a week in the buff at the El Dorado Resort and Spa. Passengers did, however, have to wait until they were on the plane before undressing — a runway full of bouncing boobs and private parts swinging in the wind wasn't part of the program. And don't start fantasizing about a little fling with the stewardess. Any kind of advances like that were strictly forbidden, and the crew, not too surprisingly, remained in uniform. Finally, no hot drinks were served on board for safety reasons. So take off your clothes and fasten your seat belts.

Did you know?

Residents of the former German Democratic Republic, where nudist vacations have long been popular, almost had their own nudist flight, thanks to the German tour operator, Ossi Urlaub. However, opponents of this kind of freedom of the skies — whose protests gave the project quite a bit of free publicity — eventually forced the company to cancel the trip, which was originally scheduled for July 2008.

Castaways Travel
PRICE: **UNAVAILABLE AT THIS TIME**
Information: **http://www.naked-air.com**

Stripped-Down Sushi

In recent years, in both Japan and China, *nyotaimori* has come back into fashion. Behind this mysterious name is an equally strange practice: a fine dining experience, composed of delicious sashimi and sushi, elegantly presented on the body of a young, naked virgin. *Nyotaimori*, sometimes called "body sushi," has been a tradition in Japan since the time of the geishas. The young women are selected for their beauty, but they also have to have incredible patience. They must remain perfectly still for several hours, no matter how their customers react. One hopes they're at least careful with their chopsticks.

Did you know?

The young woman who serves as a platter is carefully prepared before the meal, including having her skin washed with a fragrance-free soap so the taste of the food is not affected.

Body Sushi
PRICE: **ABOUT $1,000 AN EVENING**
Information: **http://www.bodysushiexperience.com**

The Love Hotels

The Caesars Pocono Resorts are the place for love — with a capital "L." At this special chain of hotels designed for cooing couples they don't do things halfway. Heart-shaped Jacuzzis and swimming pools; big, soft beds; showers for two; breakfast delivered to your room — they've thought of everything for the ultimate lovers' getaway. And you can rest assured that the hotel staff will respect the "do not disturb" sign on your door. If you want the supreme romantic experience, however, you'll have to spring for one of the suites at the chain's Pocono Palace Resort that features a whirlpool bath for two in a 7-foot (2 m) tall champagne glass. Hollywood couldn't do it better.

Did you know?

After a few trips to one or more of the group's three resorts for couples you may find yourself ready for a stay at Brookdale — the only one that accepts children.

Caesars Pocono Resorts
PRICE: **ABOUT $300 A NIGHT**
Information: **http://www.caesarspoconoresorts.com**

A Dog's Life

What are Dennis and Frances passionate about? Dogs! And it doesn't matter whether they're stuffed toys or made out of wood or metal or the real, living, barking animals. To enlarge their collection they started sculpting them out of wood — and, in order not to waste time, they use chainsaws. The next step was a bed and breakfast — a gigantic beagle that guests enter from its second-story deck. Besides the main bedroom there's a smaller loft room in the dog's head. This wooden wonder has a full bath and kitchen area and is decorated — you guessed it — with a tasteful canine theme. And you won't have to worry about being kept awake at night: this is a big dog, but it's as quiet as a mouse.

Dog Bark Park Inn Bed & Breakfast
PRICE: **ABOUT $90 A NIGHT**
Information: **http://www.dogbarkparkinn.com**

My Lovable, Insufferable Cat

Her long, thick fur is so beautiful. It's so soft and shiny. And it sets off my darn allergies! Before, cat lovers plagued by sneezing fits and teary eyes had to resort to antihistamines if they wanted to live in harmony with their favorite feline. But now Lifestyle Pets has come up with scientifically improved cats whose saliva contains almost none of the protein that triggers allergic reactions. Kitty can lick herself from head to paw without creating a health hazard. You can cuddle cheek-to-cheek, rub noses or muss up her fur and nothing dire will happen. It's cat heaven.

Did you know?

The development of the hypoallergenic cat by Lifestyle Pets, a San Diego company, is the result of years of research. In fact, *Time* magazine included the Allerca cat on its list of Best Inventions of 2006. Potential customers should be aware, however, that people with acute allergies might still find this new miracle breed something to sneeze at.

Allerca
PRICE: **FROM $5,900 TO $28,000**
Information: **www.allerca.com**

Puppy Love

Thanks to the Internet you've finally found the man of your dreams. But now you've been shamelessly ignoring your favorite pet, who is starting to let you know it. Luckily there's an animal lover out there who's come up with a great idea. The Pets-Dating site can help you find the perfect mate for Fido or Fluffy, and the service is open to all kinds of pets: dogs, cats, hamsters, mules — you name it. Pretty soon the two happy couples will each be cooing in their corners — and no more jealousy.

Pets Dating
Information: **http://www.dogster.com**

The Portable Church

" **I**f you can't get people to come to church, then take the church to the people." That's the motto of Michael Gill, inventor of the first inflatable church. Designed to be in tune with the 21st century, this portable church is delivered by truck and can be set up wherever you like. About 16 feet (5 m) wide with a 40-foot (12 m) tower, it can hold 60 people. This church has everything you'd find in a real place of worship: inflatable pews, organ, pulpit, gothic arches and colorful "stained glass" windows. The beautiful gray PVC church can be put up in about two hours, with the actual inflation taking only about 10 minutes. And the whole thing can be disassembled in just an hour.

Did you know?

People and organizations in over 20 countries have shown interest in this product, and there are now plans for inflatable mosques, synagogues and even bars.

The Inflatable Church
PRICE: **ABOUT $4,000 FOR A DAILY RENTAL, WITH A PURCHASE PRICE OF $43,500**
Information: **http://www.inflatablechurch.com**

"Amen" to this Drink

Drinking and driving is not a good idea, but drinking and praying — especially when it's water — is something else entirely. So that the faithful can be closer to God in their everyday lives, the Spiritual Brands company launched a new product, Spiritual Water. It's a bottle of purified water with colorful images of Christ, the Virgin Mary and other religious figures on the label. As a bonus there's also a prayer or inspirational message on the back. There are 11 different styles so you can vary your pleasure and your moral uplift. And this religious experience is available in bulk: the company offers cases of 24 bottles so you'll never run out of spirituality. Eight glasses a day will keep you pure in mind and pure in body.

Did you know?

The Spiritual Water line is clearly aimed at Christians, but Muslims and Jews needn't worry. The company has plans to develop new products designed especially for them.

Spiritual Water
PRICE: **$2.50 A BOTTLE**
Information: **http://spiritualh2o.com**

This Is My Toast

Miracles are getting rarer and rarer these days, and the Virgin Mary isn't exactly making daily public appearances. So it's time to react — starting with breakfast. Thanks to the Holy Toast bread stamper, with the application of just a little pressure you can mark an outline of the mother of Jesus on a slice of bread. Then all you have to do is slip it into the toaster. When it pops up you'll have her divine image burned into the toast — or lightly "browned in" if you've got the setting adjusted right. It's not exactly the Shroud of Turin, but it doesn't require any praying either — just a toaster. You can perform your own endless multiplication of the miracle, as long as someone else takes care of the multiplication of bread. These images of the Virgin Mary, however, are likely to disappear rather quickly — first under a layer of jelly or jam, and then in your mouth. Take, eat; this is my toast.

Holy Toast
PRICE: **ABOUT $4.95**
Information: **http://www.mcphee.com/**

eBay

Going, Going, Going... Mad

Nothing is lost; nothing is really created; everything in the universe just gets transformed into something else and ends up for sale on eBay. Legend has it that it was to help his sweetheart build up her collection of PEZ dispensers that the Franco-American-Iranian Pierre Omidyar came up with the idea for an Internet auction site. That was in 1995, and at the time it was called Auctionweb. Everything moved along pretty quickly, and about a year later it was renamed eBay, becoming one of the best-known and most profitable sites on the web. Today the company has about 13,000 employees, annual

You like toast, but the Virgin Mary isn't your cup of tea? Were you thinking more along the lines of sharing the breakfast, and saliva, of your favorite movie star? No problem — you can find virtually anything on the Internet, like a half-eaten piece of Justin Timberlake's toast, which one of his fans bought for $3,100. Just imagine what the price would be if they were selling the chance to put just a little piece of Justin himself between your teeth.

Suri's First Poop

In April 2006 Tom Cruise and Katie Holmes became the proud parents of a little girl named Suri. But for several months Suri remained out of the public eye, which led to some wild rumors. Luckily, in August, the artist Daniel Edwards — already known for his sculptures of Britney Spears giving birth and Paris Hilton on an autopsy table — reassured the entire world by revealing his work featuring the bronzed first poop of little Suri. The sculpture was exhibited at a New York gallery and then put up for sale on eBay, with the bid starting at $5,000. Proceeds from the sale were contributed to the March of Dimes charity organization.

After the Sandwich Man, the Forehead Woman

To help finance her son's education, American Kari Smith auctioned off her forehead as an advertising space. For $15,000 this resident of Utah now has a beautiful little tattoo with the name of an online casino on her face. Since then, a resident of Nebraska also put his head up for sale and received no less than $37,375 to turn it into an advertisement for an anti-snoring medicine. No news on whether or not Kari has decided to let her bangs grow.

for sale

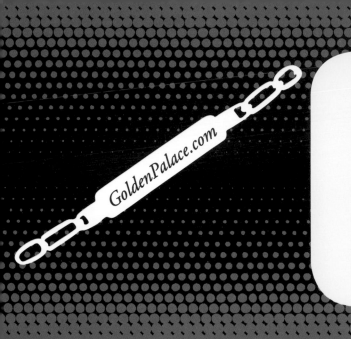

You Name It

You don't choose what country you're born in, or your family — and sometimes your parents don't even choose your first name. That's what happened to a baby born in 2005. His mother auctioned off the right to decide what her child would be called, which is how the same casino that had its name tattooed on the forehead of a woman in Utah obtained the immense pleasure of being able to name the lucky baby GoldenPalace.com for the modest sum of $15,100. The mother claims that it'll help her afford outfits and other needed items for the baby. That perhaps should include saving for future psychiatrist's bills.

Prayers for Sale

Charity isn't what it used to be. Capitalism has entered the heart of religion, at least in one Christian family which offers — or rather auctions off — its services on eBay. The high bidder will benefit from a daily prayer said by the entire family as it gathers around the Bible. All subjects of prayer are welcome, and the bidding begins at the very modest price of $100. Despite what appears to be a real bargain, so far no one has bid. Maybe it's just a little too easy. After all, no pain, no gain.

Get a Life

Your wife is getting old, your kids are driving you crazy, you're fed up with your friends and your apartment is depressing. Why not change everything? Now there's a solution: buy a whole new life. Last year on eBay a 24-year old Australian auctioned off his old socks, his scooter and his surfboard, as well as his parents, his ex-girlfriend, 8 potential replacements for her, 15 friends, 170 acquaintances, 2 enemies, his telephone number and even his name. The whole lot went for $4,800. Since then, an Irishman and another Australian have also decided to sell their lives, but this time they went a bit further and threw in their job and apartment.

sales of over $7 billion dollars, 83 million active members and, above all, no less than 600 million objects sold each year. Everything from rare finds to the most common everyday items, from valuable merchandise to bargain basement junk — and then there's a lot of really bizarre stuff. A whole lot of it — flu microbes that made Paul McCartney have to cancel a concert, a piece of chewing gum right out of Madonna's mouth, the pregnancy test kit used by Britney Spears that someone dug out of the trash can of a hotel room, a half-eaten bacon-lettuce-and-tomato sandwich belonging to the very same Britney (which sold for about $15,000), a french fry that looks like Abraham Lincoln, a cheese sandwich with the image of the Virgin Mary, a mother-in-law in perfectly good working order — including nightly snoring — dating from 1930, an old, deserted town in Texas, and the list goes on and on. Outlandish objects create a real buzz but don't always find a buyer. Because even if there's a sucker born every minute, they aren't all bidding on eBay.

The Plastic Nursery

You never get tired of doting on Jordan, your adorable little baby? Is he growing up too fast? Then order a copy! Custom-made reborn baby dolls are designed to look as realistic as possible. Everything about them — the materials used, their weight and the positions you can put them in — makes them look just like your own precious darling. Careful attention is paid to skin texture, veins and your baby's specific coloring. The hair is implanted one follicle at a time then washed and cut. Certain models even come with beating hearts. Really.

Did you know?

Reborn baby dolls are considered by some as a genuine art form, and most of them are custom-made by practicing artists. These unique creations are sometimes used in movies or special photo shoots.

Reborn Baby Dolls
PRICE: **BETWEEN $70 AND $500**
Information: **http://www.reborn-baby.com**

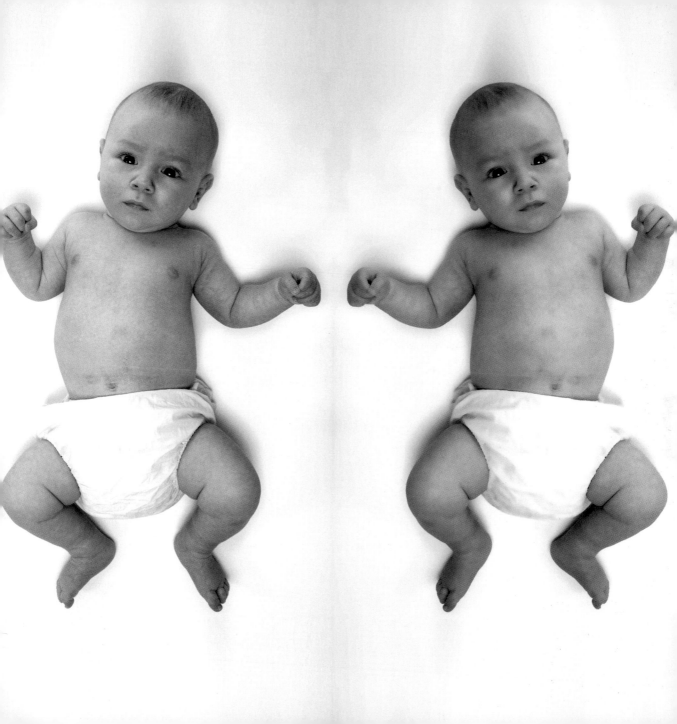

Bulletproofing Baby

Pull down your baby's bomb-resistant blanket and take him out of his bulletproof crib. Put on her camouflage overalls and jacket, and don't forget the matching helmet and bib. Then you can put your little darling in his antiballistic stroller and fit him with his baby gas mask, just in case there's a chemical attack. And just to be sure, you'd better arm yourself with a taser pistol before you head out to the park. Bullet Proof Baby is a company specializing in the protection of infants and small children, offering a variety of products to help keep them safe 24 hours a day. You'll be relieved to know, however, that none of the products offered for sale really exist. This "viral" website, with its strong dose of black humor, was part of a promotional campaign for a movie.

Bullet Proof Baby Industries
AVAILABILITY: "OUT OF STOCK"
Information: **http://www.bulletproofbaby.net**

Baby Overboard

Your baby's finally arrived, and guess what wonderful gift comes with the eight cases of powdered milk you just bought? A beautiful "Baby on Board" sticker for your car that doubles as an advertisement for the company. Not only is it totally pointless, but it'll also prove impossible to remove if you ever realize just how much you don't need it. "Brat on Board" is a whole different thing. It humorously informs other drivers, who will no doubt do a double take, that you're doing your best to stay on the road in spite of the out-of-control kids in your car. This adorable baby doll that looks like it's screaming at the top of its lungs can be hung on any of your car's side windows. A little yellow panel in the classic "Baby on Board" style is clipped to its shirt. But this one reads: "Brat on Board." With this little darling clutching the window and looking like it's desperately trying to escape from your vehicle, your fellow drivers are likely to give you a wide berth.

Brat on Board
PRICE: **ABOUT $10**
Information: **http://www.prankplace.com**

Saturday Afternoon Fever

Lucy leaves the nightclub at four o'clock — a bit tipsy, but happy. She's been shaking her booty with her friends to the beat of disco hits from the 70s and 80s mixed by a DJ who knows his stuff. The bubble machines and drinks "on the rocks" made it the perfect dance session — but now Lucy's tired and she needs a nap. At Baby Loves Disco, the atmosphere is as hip as anywhere else, but the evenings are already over at the end of the afternoon, the parking lot is full of strollers, the drinks are all fruit juices and the bathrooms are equipped with diaper changing stations. That's because Baby Loves Discos are designed for parents and their children from six months to seven years old.

Baby Loves Disco
PRICE: **ABOUT $10 TO $15 DEPENDING ON THE VENUE**
Information: **http://www.babylovesdisco.com**

Chase Teenagers Away with a New Pitch

They're young and cool and hang out in front of your store. You'd like to drive them away and leave room for a slightly older, calmer and more-likely-to-buy clientele. A British security systems company has invented a new method of chasing away the under-20 crowd with sound. Mosquito is an alarm that produces a buzzing sound similar to that of an insect. Its high pitch is inaudible to mature ears, but teenagers can hear this 18 to 20 kHz sound only too well. It takes about 8 to 10 minutes, according to the product's manufacturer, Compound Security, before the pain in their ears gets the kids to buzz off.

Did you know?

In Great Britain the Mosquito is used in public places such as the Wyvern Theatre in Swindon, but English teenagers are putting the system to a different use. They've recorded the sound and are using it as an "anti-old-people" ring tone, inaudible to adults. Maybe that's just deserts since when the inventor of the Mosquito, Howard Stapleton, was developing the product, he tested it on his own children.

Mosquito
PRICE: **ABOUT $750**
Information: **www.compoundsecurity.co.uk**

Like the Back of Your Hand

Hands can be so expressive. And if they can't exactly recite epics or stories of fantastic quests, they can carry ads. The American company Handvertising has developed a new concept to get the message of advertisers into the hands of potential customers: by putting it on the hands of potential customers. The idea is that since bars and nightclubs often stamp the hands of their customers anyway for readmittance or proof of age, why not turn these appendages into mini-billboards. So instead of a little flower or fish as a souvenir of their evening, customers' hands will display the slogan, "This is my Coca-Cola hand" or the logo of a local radio station or the name of a brand of whiskey.

Handvertising
PRICE: **CONTACT THE COMPANY FOR AN ESTIMATE**
Information: **http://www.handvertisingusa.com**

RFID Implants

You've no doubt heard about the electronic implants designed to facilitate the identification of dogs. Since 2004 this updated version of the ID tattoo is available for humans. In Mexico more than a thousand people already have radio-frequency identification (RFID) tags implanted under their skin. In theory these implants are designed for emergency situations. In the case of an accident, first-aid workers have immediate access to complete medical files, phone numbers of next of kin and details about your medical insurance. And the RFID craze doesn't stop there. The tags are also being used as a method to identify VIP customers in exclusive nightclubs. It ensures they get good service — and also allows waiters to verify the balance in their account before they bring them drinks. RFID tags can also be used to keep track of your children: special security sensors will be able to detect their presence, allowing you to know exactly where they are at any given moment.

Did you know?

Some researchers claim that RFID implants increase the risk of getting cancer. As far as invasion of privacy goes, there aren't any statistics on that yet.

RFID Implants
PRICE: **AVAILABLE UPON REQUEST**
Information: **http://www.rfidgazette.org**

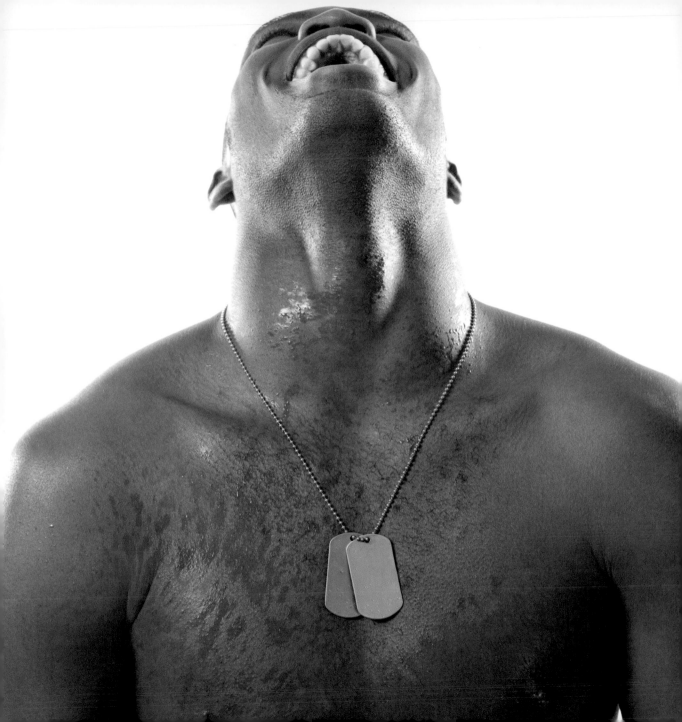

Laughing off the Enemy

Lethal weapons aren't very funny. They not only kill, they wound, maim and paralyze. Can the Laughing Bullet stop an enemy with tender loving care? Maybe not, but at least it takes a novel approach. For a while the Pentagon considered using these bullets, which release laughing gas upon impact. Hours of chuckling and snorting down in the war zone? Guerilla insurgents cracking up at the sight of their attackers? The verdict is still out. In the end, the idea, developed by California-based Agentai Inc., was abandoned, but there's still the much less humorous project of projectiles that release paralyzing — or extremely bad smelling — gas. Battlefields never were much to laugh about.

Laughing Bullet
AVAILABILITY: **PRODUCT NOT AVAILABLE**
Information: **http://www.engadget.com**

Paralyzing Music

Finally, a taser for music lovers. Just imagine... you're walking along a deserted city street at dusk, minding your own business and listening to your favorite tune as you're scrolling through the selections to see what you want to hear next — when someone tries to attack you. You're going to have to put away that music gadget and get ready to defend yourself quickly. Unless you've got a Taser MPH (Music Player Holster). This little two-in-one invention combines an MP3 player with a taser packing 50,000 volts, allowing you to paralyze your attacker without missing a beat.

Did you know?

This indispensable electronic defense device comes with its own holster and is available in pink, red and leopard motif.

Taser MPH
PRICE: **ABOUT $380**
Information: **http://www2.taser.com**

A Swiss Army of Functions

A nail file? It's got it. A fish scaler? Got that too. And then there's a magnifying glass, a cigar cutter, a can opener, a nail clipper, a reamer, scissors, a laser pointer, pliers, screwdrivers and blades, lots of blades. Designed by Wenger, the creator of the world-renowned Swiss Army Knives, the Giant Knife includes 87 different tools offering 141 functions. With all that, it's probably better to carry it in its presentation box than your pocket.

Did you know?

The Wenger Giant Knife is listed in the *Guinness Book of World Records* as the "Most Functional Penknife."

Wenger Giant Knife
PRICE: **ABOUT $877**
Information: **http://www.wenger.ch**

The Sweet Sound of Revenge

Judging from the constant racket coming from their apartment every evening, you might think your neighbors are deaf. This new CD is a good way to find out for sure. In the venerable tradition of an eye for an eye and a tooth for a tooth, it'll treat them to a wide range of pleasant sounds: a drill, a barking dog, a crying baby and many other melodious pleasures. The CD comes with a pair of earplugs so you won't hear your neighbors banging on your walls or ringing your doorbell.

Revenge CD
PRICE: ABOUT $8
Information: **http://www.wishingfish.com**

Building
on a Dream

Skyscrapers that dance, houses that like to play pranks, and shipping containers that take on a second life. They're rebelling against classic colors, defying logic and leaving rectangles to the past. Buildings are rounding off their angles and bringing a new message to humanity, sometimes in forms that make them look like they've sprung right out of a child's dreamworld. Their structures are artsy and surprising, funny and clever. And they slope or twist and take on bright colors and bold symbols. Round, oval, warped or soaring, our living and working spaces are moving into the world of tomorrow in order to make them more in harmony with those who use them.

Dancing with Fred and Ginger
The dancing house in Prague symbolizes the city's break with its totalitarian past and its desire to find a new equilibrium.
Dancing House

The Crooked House
No, you haven't been drinking. You're just at the Crooked House in Sopot, Poland.
Crooked House

Judging by the Cover
The Kansas City Public Library gives books a place of honor. That's not too surprising for a library, but its role as guardian of the city's book collection is on full display: the front of its parking garage is covered with a row of huge book spines that make it look like some giant's bookshelf.
Kansas City Library
http://kclibrary.org

Containing the Student Housing Problem

In response to a shortage of apartments, the city of Amsterdam has come up with a new idea: it's begun housing students in shipping containers. Modular, mobile and above all economic, there are now 1,500 students living in these customized units. Piled on top of each other, these 8½ by 40 foot (2.5 by 4 m) containers have been given a new role in life and a fresh coat of paint. Their colorful walls brighten up one of the old, abandoned waterfront areas in Amsterdam, which has taken on the look of a small, thriving town with a café and supermarket made out of the same materials. Tempohousing, the company in charge of the project, is on the up and up. They've recently got an order for a three-star hotel in Nigeria — also made out of containers.

Did you know?

The rent might be cheap, but this type of housing does have its drawbacks. Students have been complaining about noise and cold, the result of insufficient insulation.

Tempohousing Construction Systems
PRICE: **$27,550 PER MODIFIED CONTAINER; $363 MONTHLY RENTAL FEE**
Information: **http://www.tempohousing.com**

The House that Keeps You on Your Toes

Shusaku Arakawa and Madeline Gins have been working on the problem of the aging Japanese society. Reversible Destiny Lofts, one of their projects, were designed to stimulate the physical and mental health of their inhabitants by preventing them from falling into an unvarying routine. These constructions include bright colors and are made out of unusual materials, continually confronting those living in them with the unexpected. The floors aren't always perfectly flat, and some of the doorways are so narrow you almost have to squeeze your way through. There aren't any closets (so you have to figure out your own solution to storage problems), and good luck finding the light switches. These houses give the expression "the game of life" a whole new meaning.

Reversible Destiny Lofts
PRICE: **ABOUT $750,000 PER APARTMENT**
Information: **http://www.reversibledestiny.org**

Athletic Ironing

Think ironing is a boring household chore? It isn't for extreme ironing enthusiasts! The goal of this sport is to iron as neatly as possible in places and positions that are almost impossible. Iron while riding a bike or suspended in mid-air or on the roof. Or do it underwater, in a hot-air balloon or on a cow. Just take an iron, an ironing board and your imagination, and you're on your way. But do be careful, ironing can be more dangerous than you think.

Did you know?

The first (and so far the only) extreme ironing world championship was held in 2002 in Germany. Other planned competitions, deemed too dangerous, have had to be canceled.

Extreme Ironing
Information: http://www.extremeironing.com

Please Bathe Responsibly

At the Chodovar Brewery in the Czech Republic, the beer really flows. Besides a hotel, restaurant and, of course, bar on the premises, there's a beer spa where you can be immersed in a bath filled with a mixture of sparkling mineral water, beer, yeast, hops and crushed herbs. According to the director, the 93°F (34°C) beer bath has curative properties. This miraculous liquid softens and purifies the skin. It also provides important vitamins and can help treat acne and reduce cellulite. And even if you've already got skin as soft as a baby's, this slightly alcoholic bath also helps soothe muscles and joints and actually improves the body's immune system. Comfortably lying back in this warm, magical fluid for a relaxing 20 minutes, you can sip on a glass of nonpasteurized Rock Lager, recommended by the spa as especially beneficial for the digestive system. Warning: this kind of bathing can be addictive.

Did you know?

Beer spas also exist in Austria (www.moorhof.com) and Germany (www.bierschwimmbad.com).

The Real Beer Spa at the Chodovar Brewery
PRICE: **ABOUT $29 FOR A BATH; $12 TO $22 FOR A MASSAGE**
Information: **http://www.chodovar.cz**

The Instant Four-Leaf Clover

Everybody knows about the luck of a four-leaf clover. But when you think that there are about 10,000 of the three-leaf variety for every four-leaf treasure, you realize that you could spend a long time crawling on your hands and knees in bucolic fields before luck comes your way. Not to worry. Now you can order your very own four-leaf clover over the Internet. The special bulb comes in a mini terra cotta pot — all you have to do is add water and watch it grow. Purists claim that only four-leaf clovers found in nature "the old-fashioned way" bring good luck, but if you're a little too busy — or lazy — for that, why not give this a try?

Four-Leaf Clover
PRICE: **ABOUT $6.50**
Information: **http://www.iwantoneofthose.com**

Your Own Versailles

Transforming your scruffy little backyard into a formal French garden is child's play with this set of artificial grass mats in various curling shapes. All you do is place them on your lawn for about two weeks in any pattern you like. When you take them off your pathetic patch of weeds will become an elegant arabesque fit for the grounds of a château. And the kids can still play ball in the yard since there aren't any flowers or bushes to step on. Now even the laziest gardener in the world can compete with Louis XIV.

Did you know?

You can get personalized mats to print the message, image or logo of your choice on your lawn.

Jardin à la Française Decorating Kit
PRICE: **ABOUT $65**
Information: **http://www.rlos-design.com**

Marked by the Sun

Your guy doesn't want to get a tattoo? Even though you've explained to him how sexy you think it'd make him look? Then get him a tattooing swimsuit. Not to worry! This isn't swimwear lined with nasty-looking, ink-filled needles — it's just made out of a revolutionary new material that allows the tanning rays of the sun to pass through certain parts of it. So now while he's helping the kids build a sand castle, there'll also be a scorpion slowly appearing on his butt. Nice.

Did you know?

The Taiwanese artist Yu-Chiao Wang has created a stencil robe which, when you wear it in the sun, leaves your back marked with a large arabesque tattoo.

Tattoo System
PRICE: **FROM $72**
Information: **http://www.swimwear.es**

The Jealousy Generator

Do you feel like you've got too much freedom in your relationship? Would you like your other half to be just a bit more possessive? According to designer Björn Franke, jealousy can serve "to bolster self-esteem or to test the strength of partnerships." That's why he came up with the Imaginary Affair kit, comprised of a specially designed set of tools and accessories to make it look as though you're involved in an extramarital relationship. You can simulate bite marks, hickeys and carpet burns as well as leave traces of lipstick, perfume and hair in strategic places on your clothes or body. It's a sure way to find out just how much your partner really loves you — though if you decide to play a game like this, you may very well end up single.

Traces of an Imaginary Affair
PRICE: **PRODUCT STILL IN DEVELOPMENT**
Information: **http://www.bjornfranke.com**

The Inflatable Boyfriend

According to a recent study, many women in London are uncomfortable driving alone at night. Sheila's Wheels, a company specializing in car insurance for women, has come up with a new concept: Buddy, the inflatable man. He's not on the market yet, but the idea has received an enthusiastic reception among London's female population. Buddy, who never complains, can be stored in the glove compartment and, when needed, be inflated using a built-in pump that plugs into the car's cigarette lighter — creating the impression of a reassuring masculine presence. He just may be the man of your dreams!

Buddy
PRICE: **PRODUCT STILL IN DEVELOPMENT**
Information: **www.sheilaswheels.com**

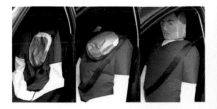

Dangerous Diamonds

It's a diamond with a killer's heart. Mounted upside down, this solitaire engagement ring invented by the designer Tobias Wong is a love token with a ferocious character. The beautiful and cruel point of the hardest stone in the world allows you to etch passionate messages in the bathroom mirror, but it can also become a sharp weapon. With a symbol of your wedding vows like this, promise yourselves you'll never fight. It'll be for better, rather than for — much — worse.

Did you know?

Another invention, the Stunning Ring, comes equipped with a button you can push if someone threatens you. In an instant, extremely strong pepper spray will squirt out, burning the eyes and taking the breath away from your assailant. And don't worry, there's a safety catch to prevent you from accidentally spraying yourself while scratching your nose.

Killer Ring
PRICE: **AVAILABLE ON REQUEST**
Information: **http://www.brokenoff.com**

War with a Feminine Touch

Is pink your little girl's favorite color? And does she not seem very interested in firearms? That's all quite normal — but does it leave you concerned about her safety? The parody website Glamguns was created for people just like you. Glambo, as the female U.S. Army veteran who founded the site calls herself, claims that she wants to shake up female stereotypes with her products. A Hello Kitty AK-47, a My Little Pony M4A1 carbine, a Lady Di Smith & Wesson handgun or antipersonnel mines in Martha Stewart colors are just some of the humorous — and insane — customized weapons for sale. If you're forced to take prisoners you can keep them under control with a pair of Paris Hilton handcuffs. And Glamguns hasn't forgotten the moms. They also offer the Motha T, a shoulder-fired rocket launcher inspired by Mother Theresa. The website offers on-line purchasing, but don't bother ordering — none of it is real.

Glamguns
AVAILABILITY: **NEVER**
Information: **http://www.glamguns.com**

Absolutely Nothing

What can you give someone who already has 19 sweaters and 4 wallets? What about millions of protons and billions of neutrons? There's abundance in emptiness, or, as the saying goes, "less is more." This sphere of nothing — except, that is, for a little bit of air and wit — is the perfect gift for those who already have it all. It's a nothing full of philosophy; a nothing you've just got to have; a nothing that seems to include everything — and that you can't find anywhere else.

Nothing
PRICE: **ABOUT $7.25**
Information: **http://www.iwantoneofthose.com**

places

toys

ideas

world

Photo Credits